LESSONZ LEARNED

by

She216

Copyright © 2019 She216

All rights reserved.

ISBN: 978-1-7348607-4-0

"IF YOU WALKED BY A STREET AND YOU WAS WALKING ON CONCRETE AND YOU SAW A ROSE GROWING FROM CONCRETE, EVEN IF IT HAD MESSED UP PETALS AND IT WAS A LITTLE TO THE SIDE YOU WOULD MARVEL AT JUST SEEING A ROSE GROW THROUGH CONCRETE. SO WHY IS IT THAT WHEN YOU SEE SOME GHETTO KID GROW OUT OF THE DIRTIEST CIRCUMSTANCES AND HE CAN TALK AND HE CAN SIT ACROSS THE ROOM AND MAKE YOU CRY, MAKE YOU LAUGH, ALL YOU CAN TALK ABOUT IS MY DIRTY ROSE, MY DIRTY STEMS AND HOW I'M LEANING CROOKED TO THE SIDE. YOU CAN'T EVEN SEE THAT I'VE COME UP FROM OUT OF THAT SHIT."

- TUPAC SHAKUR

Dear Mama

I know that both of you are truly disgusted with me! You had so many high expectations, and you definitely didn't raise me to be the way I've turned out to be. I'm fifteen years old and I have a newborn baby that I can't even take care of! I don't know how to be a mom or how to provide for myself! Mama, I'm so sorry for everything! I'm sorry I stole from you, snuck out of the house, and I'm sorry that I didn't keep my virginity! I feel like I can never be the daughter that you want! When you and Daddy sent me away to that detention home, I lost my mind! The correctional officer yelled at me every day in that place! I know y'all were hurt and upset that your teenage daughter was pregnant. And you didn't want anybody to know because you were embarrassed! But you sent me away like a caged animal, away from everything and everybody! I cried every day and night while I was there and y'all barely came to visit me! But I think I know what the problem is. You wish I were more like Denise! She's smart, responsible, and not hanging out in these streets like me. Daddy won't even talk to me, and it's killing me inside! I just want to hear his voice, and hear him say I'm still his little girl! I'm going to make things a lot easier for everyone though. I'm running away! I can't take care of Sheila right now. But once I

get on my feet, I will come back for her! You know I love my baby so much, but I know both of you can provide a much better home for her than I ever could. Chauncey hasn't called me in weeks, and I haven't seen him since Sheila was born! So please, keep Sheila away from him, he doesn't deserve to see her. I love you Mama, I love you Daddy. Please forgive me, and take care of my baby!"
  Your daughter,
  Sasha

  Sasha folded the letter in half, stuffed it in an envelope, and signed her name on it. Then she took her three-month old baby and put her in the car seat with the letter. Sheila's rose-colored cheeks were glowing. Sasha could always make her little face just light up, smiling from ear to ear. She took the car seat that Sheila was sitting in and sat it on top of the kitchen table. Then she leaned over to kiss her baby on the forehead and instantly became physically weak. Sasha was full of despair and grief because she didn't want to leave her baby. Tears fell from her face onto Sheila's cheek and ended up on her little chest. Sasha turned away and walked out the door. All while her baby was left on the table helpless, watching her mother walk away from her...

***

  It was September of 1985 and *Facts of Life* was the latest new hit TV show. *Tootie, Natalie is going to go crazy when she finds out what you did!* Denise thought in regards to the show... *Ah man, it's already six o'clock?! Let me get my ass up and do this homework, I hate chemistry!* Suddenly, there was a noise in the distant background. "Sasha, get the baby! She's up from her nap I think she needs a bottle!" A few minutes went by, but still no response from Sasha... "Sasha get the baby, don't you hear her crying!?" But still, there was no answer from Sasha. "What type of mother are you, letting your baby cry for this long, really Sasha?!" Denise yelled out from downstairs. She assumed that Sasha was upstairs in her bedroom ignoring the baby. She quickly got up and walked towards her crying niece. She was led into the kitchen where she discovered Sheila on top of a table sitting in her car seat. And she was crying hysterically. *What in the hell is going on?!* Denise was in disarray at what she saw. She ran to the table and unhooked her niece from the car seat. *Oh my goodness, what are you doing here all by yourself!?...Wait, what's this?* Denise looked down and noticed the letter Sasha left inside of the car seat. She sat down with her niece on her lap and began to read it...

After reading the letter, Denise furiously threw it down on the table and burst out into tears. *Why would she do this, what in the hell is wrong with her?! She just left her baby here helpless and all alone? This girl has completely lost her damn mind!* Denise was on a rant and questioned her sister's actions. Scrambling to collect her thoughts, she tried to figure out what she should do next... *Oh my goodness, ok, what should I do? I know, I'll call Mama!* She scurried to get to her feet while holding Sheila in her arms. Then she picked up the phone to call Nora...

"Hello, Ma?!"

"Hey Denise, is everything ok? Why do you sound so nervous?"

"Mama, Sasha just ran away from home! She left Sheila all alone in her car seat on top of the kitchen table, and she's gone, she just left!"

"Wait a minute, what do you mean she ran away?! Are you two in some sort of trouble, where is your sister?!"

"Ma I just told you she ran away! She left a stupid letter in the baby's car seat saying all this mess about her leaving because she can't take care of her!"

"Denise, I'm on my way. I'm coming home right now! You just wait there with the baby for me!"

Denise began to cry. "Ok Ma, I'm really scared though, where do you think she went?!"

"Sweetie just let me get home ok. We'll sort this whole thing out once I get there, I promise!"

"Ok Ma, see you in a little while!"

Nora hung up the phone. "Lord, where on earth is my child!?!...

***

Nora made it home twenty minutes later. She was struck with anxiety as soon as she walked into the house. "Give me the baby! And where is the letter?" Denise gave the baby and the letter to Nora. She sat down and began to read it...

"Isn't she worried about what could happen to her?! She must think those gang bangers she hanging with will help her! The only thing they're going to help her with is to a quick death!" While bashing her daughter's ruthless actions, Nora's eyes became filled with tears. Denise took hold of her hand for support.

"Ma, it's going to be ok! She has to be somewhere around the neighborhood. With no money or car she can't get that far!" Suddenly, Nora's husband came rushing through the door. She called him while she was on her way home and told him everything that happened. "Where is Sasha?!" He asked in a vigorous and angry tone. Frank was a tall cocky man with broad shoulders. He had the type of look that demanded respect. And no one ever dared to challenge him if they knew what was best for them...

"Where is she?! And what were you talking about on the phone Nora?! All this shit about Sasha running away and leaving the baby?!" He went to his granddaughter while she was in Nora's arms and kissed her on the forehead. Sheila was the only one that could bring out his gentle side.

"Frank I just got here, we're still trying to figure everything out baby! I think Sasha has gone completely crazy this time!" Nora gave Frank Sasha's letter so he could read it.

"Denise what happened, did you see her before she left?"

"No Ma I didn't! I was in the living room watching TV. She must have left during that time."

"Did she tell you she was going anywhere today?"

Denise tried to remember if Sasha mentioned anything about going out. "You know what, I think I overheard her on the phone this morning with Carmilla. She was saying something about going to the mall to look for an outfit for homecoming. Maybe they're at the mall!"

Frank abruptly interrupted the conversation after reading the letter… "I swear, when I find this girl, I'm going to beat the hell out of her! Maybe she'll learn some common sense then!" He bawled up the letter and threw it on the ground. "She's got everybody worried sick about her while she's out here with these damn low life ass thugs who don't give a damn about her!" Frank stormed off upstairs.

"Ma, Daddy can't just jump to conclusions like that! I mean she might not necessarily be with the Bloods. Let's go see if Carmilla-"

Denise stopped in mid statement as her attention was turned towards her father who was coming back down the stairs holding a 357 special revolver gun in his right hand.

Nora gasped in fear. "Frank, what are you doing with that gun?!"

"I'm going to get my daughter back! I know she's with those gang banging Bloods hanging out over there on Shaw! I'm driving over there, and if they don't tell me where she is, then they'll have hell to pay!"

Nora got up from her seat and passed the baby to Denise. "Take the baby upstairs and let me talk to your father in private." Denise hurried up the stairs with her niece in her arms.

"Look Frank, I know you're upset! But baby we have to think logically and smart! I called the police but -"

"Those bastards said she has to be missing for 24 hours! Forget waiting on the police Nora! What if that was their daughter missing?! They wouldn't wait 24 hours to search for her!"

"Baby I know, I know! But look, we can't handle it this way! You can't put yourself in a situation to end up in jail!"

Frank sighed heavily. "You tell me then Nora, what's the next move, huh? What are we going to do to find Sasha?!"

"Well for starters, let's not think the worst, she might not be with the Bloods. Maybe she's with Carmilla! Denise said she overheard her talking on the phone earlier about going shopping for homecoming. Let's go to Carmilla's house and see if she's there or if her family heard from Sasha. That's a good place to start baby ok, let's be smart about this. I know you're worried about her just as much as I am! But in my heart I know God is watching over her honey, I know he is!"

Frank paced the floor back and forth. He looked at Nora, and then towards the stairway. After giving it some thought, he ran upstairs to their bedroom and put his gun away. Then he went back downstairs, grabbed Nora by her waist, and kissed her on the cheek. Taking her by the hand, he led her out the door, on a search for Sasha…

I'm Leaving Everything Behind

"Who is it?"

"Carmilla, it's me Sasha, open the door!"

"Hey girl, I thought you were going to call me before you came over so I could get this hair of mine together first!" Sasha looked at Carmilla and instantly began to cry.

"Sasha, baby what's wrong?!"

Looking up with tears rushing from her hazel brown eyes, she attempted to calm herself down so that she could speak clearly. "I just can't take it anymore! I can't stand being in that house, it feels like I'm living in a prison!"

Carmilla wrapped her arm around Sasha's shoulders. "Oh no, what's wrong now? Did Nora try to lock you in the house again?"

Sasha instantly snapped. "You know what, your fucking jokes ain't funny right now! I'm on the verge of leaving Cleveland and my baby, so my life isn't a damn laughing matter!"

"Damn, I didn't mean anything by it, I'm sorry! I would never joke about anything serious you have going on! I didn't know it was, I'm just, I -" Carmilla stumbled over her speech, clearly at a loss for words.

"Girl I'm so sorry. You know I'm just really stressed out right now! This nigga Chauncey hasn't been giving me any money to help out with Sheila. And he hasn't even seen her since she was born! Worst of all, word on the streets is that he's messing around with Tameka now!"

"Tameka, girl who is that?"

"It's his next-door neighbor girl! The same chick that was telling me all last year how he was no good for me, and that I could do better!"

"Wow Sasha, she's a back stabber for doing that!"

"Yeah, well apparently she must like sloppy seconds! But who cares, she doesn't have anything on me Carmilla!" Now Sasha was what guys referred to as being a tall drink of water. And she had an hour-glass frame to go with it. A slim waist and curves shaped to perfection. Standing at 5'8", she was built like a stallion and men would call her just that, a tall stallion. She was the catch of the city, and any man that had any type of hustle about himself wanted her. From the football jocks to the dope boys, even grown ass businessmen had a thing for Sasha. But her heart belonged to Chauncey, and everyone knew it. Most people couldn't understand it, and some hated the idea of it. But above all, her parents despised it.

"Look, you don't even have the time or energy to be focused on that Sasha! You have a beautiful baby girl, Sheila is gorgeous! And what's this talk I heard you say, about leaving the city, and leaving Sheila?! Come on now girl, I know you love Chauncey and all, but that nigga is not worth you leaving your baby behind! And nothing at home could be that bad to make you want to leave your daughter! Shit, girl honestly you're talking crazy because you know I'm not letting your ass go anywhere!" The girls looked at each other and began to smile with tears in their eyes. Then they embraced one another with a hug.

"Your problems are my problems Sasha! We've been best friends since we were five years old, and you're more like a sister to me. I would never leave you hanging! We are in this together ok, that's my God child! And at the end of the day, forget Chauncey and everybody else! As long as you and Sheila are happy, then that's all that matters!"

"Carmilla, that's why I love you! And I know, talking about leaving the city and Sheila sounds crazy! I just feel like I can't handle the responsibility or the thought of being a mother! Like come on girl, we're only fifteen years old! What am I going to do with a little baby? And as fucked up as it sounds, I still want to go out and have fun! I want to do the things that make me happy! This baby is only going to slow me down... Girl, I can't even lie. Sometimes I wish I would have just given Sheila up for adoption like Chauncey wanted me to. Maybe we would still be together, maybe we would still -" Sasha stopped midway in her thoughts and slumped down onto Carmilla's bed. She grabbed a pillow and hugged it tightly as she reminisced about her child's father.

"You probably don't want to hear what I'm about to say. But I think you're being really selfish right now Sasha! You decided to have sex, so you have to deal with the responsibility of being a mother! And yeah, it's going to be extremely hard to be a mom! You have to still go to school and graduate, but you can do it! You know me and my mom are glad to help you however we can! And as much as your parents get on your nerves, they do buy everything the baby needs. And you know they love her to death! They're not going to let that baby go untaken care of! You should be focusing on you and Sheila right now! And once you stop smoking weed and hanging out with these thugs, I'm sure things will get a lot better for you."

"Look, a lot of the things you're saying are true Carmilla, ok, I'll admit that. But I don't need you telling me who to be friends with. I choose my friends just fine, I chose you didn't I? I did that without any assistance, so I know what type of company to pick for my life!"

"Don't go getting all sarcastic and defensive Sasha. I'm just saying that some of your choice of company, I mean, they're just -"

"They're just a little what Carmilla, a little hood, Ghetto, bad, a little thuggish?! What, they're not good enough for your standards little Ms. Perfect? You must be all holier than thou and shit! Oh wait, I forgot you're perfect, that's what it is! Motha fuckas kill me with that shit! Acting like they're just Saints and never did nothing wrong. You're just like my damn parents! You should have been their daughter, they'd love you! ... Damn, I just wish people really understood me sometimes."

"Sasha, I do understand you! But at the same time I just want what's best for you and the baby. Who happens to be my God Daughter by the way!"

"I know you do Carmilla."

"And speaking of my baby, where the hell is she, who has my little chunky monkey?!"

Sasha's heart felt like it had sank deep down into the pits of her stomach. Thinking of how she left Sheila on the table strapped down in her car seat with the letter. She began to second guess her decision and instantly became distraught all over again. "Oh, she's with Denise, they're at home watching *Facts of Life*. You know Denise is addicted to that damn show." The girls both laughed. "So, are we still going to the mall to find an outfit for homecoming?"

"Hell yea girl! Let me just go change my clothes real quick and I'll be ready."

"Ok," Sasha looked through some music records in Carmilla's room while waiting on her to get dressed. Suddenly, Carmilla's mom knocked on the bedroom door. "Hey Mrs. Parker, how are you?" They greeted each other with a hug.

"Hey sweetie I'm fine, just getting home from work. I can't wait to sit down and relax... Where's the baby?"

"Oh, she's at home with my sister."

"Well next time you bring her with you ok?! She's just as cute as a little button. And she looks just like you!"

Sasha forced herself to smile. She was uncomfortable with the conversation, knowing that she just left Sheila all alone. "Yes, I will surely do that Mrs. Parker, next time I won't forget."

"Ok honey. What are you and Carmilla getting ready to do?"

Carmilla entered the room at that moment. "Hey mom, we're just going to the mall to look for something to wear for homecoming."

"Oh ok, well don't get anything too tight, too short, or too low cut in the cleavage area!"

Carmilla shook her head while rolling her eyes in disagreement at her mother. Sasha couldn't stop laughing at the two go back and forth. "Ok mom, I hear you!"

***

Nora and Frank arrived at Carmilla's house thirty minutes later and knocked on the door.

"Yes, who is it?"

"Hey Bonnie, it's me Nora, I've got Frank with me. Can we talk to you for a minute?"

Bonnie was surprised to get a visit from Nora and Frank. They rarely ever came over unannounced… "Sure, come on in. Is everything ok?"

"We hope so Bonnie."

"Oh, well you actually just missed the girls, they left about thirty minutes ago."

Nora and Frank looked at each other with a smile of relief.

"What's going on?" Bonnie asked while looking confused.

"Honey I'm sorry, we're just very overjoyed right now! Sasha left a letter at home, telling us that she ran away, and that she was leaving Sheila! So we're worried about her right now! We're just glad to know that she's with Carmilla and not the wrong people!"

"My goodness, I'm so sorry I had no idea!"

"Bonnie you had no way of knowing, Nora and I are just glad she's safe. By the way, where did the girls go?"

"The girls went to the mall to look for homecoming outfits."

Frank's facial expression quickly turned into a look of aggravation. "She has the nerve to want to go shopping, after she just said she's running away from home, and leaving her baby?! Doesn't she have any remorse for what she's done?!"

"Now Frank, I know you're upset. But you can't be too hard on her! I mean she's still just a kid herself, give her a break!"

Frank stood up from where he was sitting and made direct eye contact with Bonnie. "Well Bonnie, until you have a fifteen year old daughter that gets pregnant, does drugs, and hangs out with gang members, I don't think you really have a place to comment on how I should raise my daughter!" Frank stormed out of the house.

"Bonnie, I'm so sorry about that! He's just upset about this whole thing and he doesn't really know how to deal with it!" Nora pleaded on Frank's behalf.

"Oh don't be silly, there's no need to apologize Nora! How about you make yourself comfortable here and wait for the girls to get back. I'm going up stairs, I have some things to do."

"Thanks Bonnie, I truly appreciate this. It means everything to me right now!"

"Of course Nora, anything I can do to help!"

Bonnie left Nora downstairs in the living room. She sat anxiously waiting on her daughter's return…

Things will never be the same

Sasha and Carmilla were walking on their way back home from the mall. "Girl, now you know your mom is going to be all over your ass about that sequence red dress! The draping neckline that exposes your breast, and that high split up your right thigh is going to give her a heart attack!"

"Honey please, I'm practically a grown woman! My mom will have to start accepting some things. I'm not going to be mommy's little girl forever!"

"Yeah not forever, just until you're like thirty-five!" Carmilla playfully punched Sasha on the arm.

As the two approached Carmilla's house, Frank noticed the girls from a distance while sitting in his car. He attempted to get out at first, but then he decided to wait until they got a little closer.

Meanwhile, Sasha spotted her father's car and stopped dead in her tracks. Then she grabbed Carmilla by the arm. "Girl, oh my goodness wait, stop walking! Is that my dad's car parked in the front of your house?"

Carmilla looked towards the car, trying to see if it was Frank. "Oh shit girl, I think that is your dad's car! They must be looking for you!"

"Damn, I should have never come to your house! I should have known they would try to come here looking for me! Come on, let's turn around and go back the other way!"

"Ok," Carmilla agreed.

But before they could get any further, Frank came rushing out of the car making his way towards them. "Sasha!" He yelled out to the top of his lungs. Meanwhile, Nora was in the house and heard Frank's loud voice. She quickly ran outside into the street where everyone was.

Sasha saw both of her parents approaching her and immediately felt like she was going to have an anxiety attack.

Frank instantly went into a fit of rage and yanked Sasha by her arm once he got a hold of her. "What in the hell is wrong with you?! Do you know you've got everybody worried sick? And you left the baby on top of a table all by herself?! You'll never amount to anything good in life! You aint nothing but a damn whore and I'm ashamed to even call you my daughter!"

Nora and Carmilla were in shock, fearful that Frank was going to physically attack Sasha. By this time all the neighbors had come out of their homes to witness the chaotic scene unraveling outside.

Bonnie heard the altercation inside from her bedroom window, and immediately ran outside to join the drama. Once outside she called for her daughter. "Carmilla, honey come in the house, you don't need to be a part of this crazy scene! And Frank, you're acting out of control! You need to leave with your family now or someone is going to call the police! You're making a scene and you look like a fool!"

Meanwhile, Nora was trying to grab her husband's arm, attempting to get him to loosen up his grip on Sasha. But he aggressively shrugged her off at each try. "Frank, baby Bonnie is right! This is not the place or time to do this! Look at all these people out here looking baby, you're making a scene! Let's go before somebody calls the police!" Nora pleaded desperately with Frank.

Sasha was terrified of her father. She couldn't believe that he was making a public spectacle of her in front of the entire neighborhood. She felt helpless, embarrassed, and unloved all at the same time... "This is exactly why I ran away." Sasha admitted through her sobbing cries. She could barely find the courage to speak. And her throat felt like she had swallowed a golf ball. "This is not love, you're hurting me daddy! You won't even hear anything I have to say!" Trying to choke back her tears, Sasha continued to speak, then all of a sudden three police cars pulled up.

They immediately got out of their cars with guns pointed directly at Frank. "Put your hands up now mother fucker! And let go of the girl! Step away and put your got damn hands up now ass hole!" The two white officers demanded Frank with much anger. And their faces were blood shot red.

Frank loosened his grip from Sasha's arm and took a few steps away from her. All while raising his hands high above his head in the air.

"Oh my god, no officers, please!" Nora fell to her knees. "This is my husband and he's her father!"

By this time, one of the officers grabbed Frank and hurled him down to the ground, forcing him to lay face down. Then the other officer took both of his arms, put them behind his back, and hand cuffed him. "Ma'am, you need to step away from the suspect right now!" The officer demanded Nora. She was still kneeling near Frank while he was on the ground. Nora continued to cry hysterically as she moved away from Frank and joined Sasha. "We got a call about a disturbance in the neighborhood, a possible disorderly conduct. But this looks more like domestic violence."

Frank attempted to speak. "Officer this is my daughter, she ran away from home!"

"Sir, we didn't ask for your input! You don't need to tell us anything. We saw exactly what happened with our own eyes!"

"But officer, I -"

"Now you listen here got damn it! I don't need you to say another word! You're under arrest based on the fact that we saw you assaulting your own daughter! You can explain everything to the judge you piece of shit!"

Frank was oblivious at this point.

"Officer, I swear to God there has been a huge mistake! My husband would never hurt our daughter, he was just -"

"Yea, well that's not for us to determine what started the altercation. That's for a judge and a jury to figure out. We're here to determine if there was a crime committed."

Nora looked at Sasha, then she fainted and fell to the ground.

"Mama!"

Bonnie ran to Nora's side, while Frank yelled out her name as if his life depended on it...

"Hey Charlie, this is Officer Carter. We need an ambulance right now. We have a woman down, I repeat, we have a woman down. A black female, she needs a paramedic immediately."

***

Man, this social worker is going to be all over my ass for being late, I know it! Sasha thought to herself while she was on her way to an appointment she had. Once she finally arrived, she checked in and waited for her Social Worker to come out…

"Sasha, how are you doing today?"

"Oh, I'm good Mrs. Gates."

"Well I thought something may have been wrong, since you're twenty minutes late for our appointment again."

Sasha immediately got agitated. She knew Mrs. Gates was going to get on her case about being late.

"I'm sorry Mrs. Gates, I was running late and I missed my bus, then the -"

"Sasha, you know quite frankly I'm really tired of your excuses. I mean for heaven's sake, you're someone who's trying to get their daughter back and out of foster care! But you're not putting forth much effort! I don't care what you have to do. But do whatever needs to be done to get here on time! I'm a busy woman and I don't have time to waste on a person that fits the criteria of an under achiever. You fit the statistics of someone who will only have a life expectancy of fifty years, if you're lucky! And even worse, a sixty percent chance of being incarcerated! So if you want to just give up now, then by all means please do so. Do us both a favor! Otherwise, get here on time, or I'll make recommendation to the judge for permanent placement of Sheila. Show me some effort or I'll take away any chances you have of ever getting your daughter back. Do I make myself clear?!"

Sasha looked at Mrs. Gates in disbelief. One side of her wanted to go into attack mode. While the other side of her wanted to cry on the woman's shoulder. She knew that Mrs. Gates was telling her the right thing to do. She just didn't know if she could deliver on her end. "Sure Mrs. Gates, whatever you say."…

"So let's do a little recap here. You've been working for seven months now I see. At the Burger King over on Euclid Ave., is that correct?"

"Yeah, I'm still working at that dump. And they don't pay me shit either."

"Whoa whoa whoa, wait one moment! You're going to speak with respect in my presence, do you understand me Sasha?! I know your mother didn't raise you to be this way! The era me and her grew up in, honey we couldn't even speak to an adult or an elder without saying Mrs. or Mr., let alone curse in their presence! Your mother must really be heartbroken! I mean here you are, you've lost custody of your daughter. And your poor mother is in assisted living trying to recover from a stroke that you gave her! While your father is awaiting trial, for trying to correct his unruly child the old fashioned way! Well, only God knows the truth on that one. Sasha you have practically destroyed everything and everyone around you, and it seems like you have no regards! You take everything for granted, and you don't want to do what you need to do in order to correct your wrongs! So tell me, why are you here again? I mean what's the goal that you want to accomplish, because I'm not seeing it!"

Sasha broke down into tears. She hadn't seen her father in months since the ordeal outside of Carmilla's house. And she hadn't visited her mother as much as she could have. Sasha was just about ready to let her aunt keep full custody of Sheila. At least her aunt Veronica could provide a stable home for Sheila. Mrs. Gates interrupted Sasha's thoughts…"And poor Denise, that girl is a scholar! She really works hard, trying to make something of herself. And what did you go and do? You broke up her stable home and took y'all mother and father away from her. I pray that God gives your aunt the strength to take care of Denise and that baby of yours. Because you are nowhere near ready to get back custody of Sheila! You haven't been going to your parenting classes regularly. And you're not working the mandatory twenty five hours a week like you need to. It really looks like you just don't want to succeed on purpose!"

"I do want my baby back Mrs. Gates! And don't you think I feel terrible about my mom and dad right now?" Sasha wiped the tears from her face and stood up. "I know what everything may look like, but there are a lot of things you just don't know Mrs. Gates! And I'm not making excuses. I just need a little more time to get myself together!"

"Sasha, have a seat... Listen to me. You will be eighteen in two years from now. From that point on, sweetheart your life will completely change as you know it! This teenage work program you're in, that ends once you're an adult. Where will you live once that's over? I hope you don't think your parents will take you back in, especially with your mother recovering from a stroke, if she even recovers!

Hell, she'll barely be able to care for herself! And after all this turmoil you've put your father through, causing him to lose his auto shop because he's locked up awaiting trial. You're lucky if you ever get to see his face again! Baby, you're going to get a taste of the real world as soon as you're eighteen! Personally, I think this world is going to eat you alive. And you'll end up being just another statistic. All the signs are just inevitable!"

Sasha got up from her seat again. "Well Mrs. Gates, you have your opinions and you're entitled to them."

"No Sasha these are facts, true statements, this isn't any opinion."

"Ok, well Mrs. Gates I really can't handle this negativity coming from you right now. So what else do you need from me?"

Mrs. Gates straightened the folders on her desk. Then she stood up and walked towards the door. "I'd like for you to leave Sasha."

"Wait leave, what do you mean? We didn't even have our review yet!"

"Oh, but we did! I've seen all that I need to see from you today. You have another meeting with me in three months. When you come back, I will have a decision made as to what I think should be the next step for you, and the best living situation for Sheila."

***

Sasha sat at the bus stop after leaving her appointment with Mrs. Gates. She thought about the conversation they just had. It made her feel sad as she thought about everything. Suddenly, one of the Blood gang members approached her.

"What's up Blood?" It was Mark, one of Chauncey's friends.

"What's up Blood?" Sasha instantly felt relieved when she saw him. It seemed like his company could help lift her spirits for the moment.

"Shit you know, just shooting my one two. I'm about to go and talk to these Dominicans about coping this key. What you about to get into?"

"Oh, well I have to go to work in a few hours."

"Girl why the fuck you still working at that shitty ass burger joint!?"

Sasha laughed, "You know I'm trying to get my daughter back. So I need all the money I can get right now!"

"Shit, working there you getting all the change you can get. Like nickels, quarters and dimes, not no real fucking money!" They both laughed.

"Mark, shut up!"

"Seriously though Sasha, you could be making some serious money! You already down with the crew anyway because you fucking with my nigga Chauncey."

Chauncey was one of the top dope dealers in Cleveland and one of the highest ranking Blood members. He had a lot of power and the streets respected him.

"Now Mark, you know Chauncey would flip out if he knew I was out here pushing weight!"

Mark shook his head in disagreement. "When you going to stop playing stupid? You know that nigga out here doing him and every other bitch he meet… Look, the nigga probably got love for you and all, because you had his baby. But shit Ma, you gotta do you! You gotta live right? Come on now think about it baby. This nigga got you out here riding public transportation. And you working at a burger joint. That's not a good look!" Mark really had Sasha thinking about some of the points he was making. But she didn't know if it was genuine or if he was just trying to use the situation to get close to her. She knew he had romantic interest ever sense he tried to get with her at a party last year… "I don't know Mark, I'm already in so much trouble as it is. I really don't need any more problems."

"How is making money a problem though baby? Look, you see that Benz parked over there?" Mark had a red two door drop top Benz. He was a flashy dude and always wanted to show off how much money he had. "I mean for real though, if you was my bitch, you wouldn't want for anything!"

Sasha started to blush. She always thought he was fine. She just never wanted to cross Chauncey, since he was Mark's best friend. But finding out that Chauncey had a baby on the way with

Tameka made all the rules go out the window. And anyone was fair game now.

"Yeah, tell me anything. And by the way, I'm not anybody's bitch Mark!"

"You know what I mean Ma. I don't say all that soft shit like my lady, and all that other corny shit. But aye, I need to go meet with this plug I just told you about. You trying to come with me?"

Sasha looked down at her watch, knowing she had to be at work in less than two hours. She contemplated the move. "Mark, I told you I have to go to work in a little while."

"So you really still talking about this burger joint huh? Look, just come ride with me and see what I do. I'm telling you, I can set you up with a nice position baby! You can easily make two grand a week! Just fuck with me, let me show you what I do!"

Sasha knew that type of money could help her do things a lot quicker. She could find an apartment and get back custody of Sheila. And she was thrilled at the idea of not having to work at Burger King. "I'll go Mark, but only if you promise to drop me back off at work."

"Yea ok, but when you see all this money I'm about to show you, the only time you'll be at a burger joint is to eat."...

The Game

It was 1986 and the dope game was the biggest hustle throughout inner city ghettos. You had guys under twenty five years old making at least $20k in a week. Mark had really made a name for himself, but most people just saw him as being Chauncey's wingman. So he always had this mindset that he needed to prove himself and show that he could make his own moves without Chauncey's help. On top of that, he had been crushing on Sasha for some time now, and he secretly felt that he was the better man for her...

"Alright baby, we about to go in here, and I'm about to talk with my Dominican connect. All I want you to do is sit back and look sexy Ma. It'll help me get this money a lot easier. These motha fuckas get dumb founded when they see a pretty face, you feel me?"

Sasha was a little uneasy about going inside with him. They drove about an hour outside the city and arrived at this huge gated estate. You couldn't even get past the gates without being let in by security. She always knew that Mark and Chauncey were in the dope game. But she had no idea it was to this magnitude. The house had tall white pillars at the entrance, double French doors, and a courtyard. It was all that and then some. Sasha had always dreamed of living this type of lifestyle.

"Mark, they're going to look at me and think to themselves who is this little ghetto chick coming in here with you. I don't even look like I belong in a place like this!"

"See Ma, not to be rude, but you don't get paid to think baby." Sasha shoved him on the arm. "Seriously though, you underestimate yourself too much. Probably because you use to fucking with these corny ass dudes that's not getting no money! They don't know how to take you to the next level. Like real talk Sasha, you a bad lil bitch. And if you really fucked with a nigga like me, I'd have yo shit popping, for real baby. You'd have all new everything! Never would my child's mother be riding on the bus!"

"Mark, I told you I'm not your bitch!"

"My bad sweetheart. I know how it might sound to you. But when I say it, I mean my ride or die. I look at you as a boss chick Sasha, and baby the world is yours! Shit, with a woman like you by my side, it aint no stopping me!"

Sasha looked at Mark, as if she were now under his spell or something. She had fallen for him, and everything he said made her desire him more and more. His cologne was intoxicating, and his dreamy green eyes were hypnotizing. He was built like a football player. And his muscles pierced through his shirt. His mocha colored smooth skin, brush waves, and deep voice would drive any girl crazy. And he knew he was the shit. "Mark, you know I'm really feeling what you're telling me. But you already know what it is with me and you. I just don't know what your true intentions are. And Chauncey just -"

"Aye, for real though, you shouldn't even keep talking about that nigga in my presence. I'm kind of tired of you bringing him up!" Mark slumped back in his seat and began to brush his waves.

"I'm not saying it like that Mark."

"Well how you saying it then?"

Before Sasha could answer, Mark grabbed the bottom of her face, bringing it closer to his. "Girl, I don't have time to play games with you. That's my nigga and all, but what me and you got going on don't have shit to do with him. Me and Chauncey get money together, bull shit around, and that's it! That nigga don't have no ring on you. So I'm asking, who you choosing Sasha?" Mark began kissing on her neck. The rhythmic passion of his tongue stroking on her neck made her clit wet. She couldn't believe how aroused and horny he had made her that fast.

"I'm choosing you." Sasha whispered into Mark's ear. Then he kissed her passionately on the lips. Their tongues were erotically intertwined, one with the other, in search of a never ending pleasure. He grabbed her breast with one hand, while gripping a handful of her ass with the other.

Pulling away from her embrace, Mark gazed into her eyes. "You got my dick hard as fuck! That's my pussy, and you my girl. You mines now, and that's all that need to be said. And fuck that burger joint bull shit, you not doing that no more."

Sasha didn't know what to think. She was still in a daze from the erotic moment that just took place. Then she thought about Sheila, and how desperately she wanted her back. "Look Mark I really want you, really I do, but -"

"Ain't no buts! If you fucking with me then you fucking with only me. Or if not, I can just drop you off at that weak ass burger shack."

"Mark don't be like that. You know I got a lot of fucked up shit going on right now. My parents are in a bad situation! One is sick, the other one is in jail. And I have to get back custody of my daughter!" Sasha began to cry, thinking about the state of being her family was in. It hurt her deeply and she felt responsible.

"I'm going to help you with all of that Sasha."

Sasha looked up at him with tears in her eyes. Mark took his thumb and wiped the tears from her face. "Baby I got you! I'm not going to hurt you! I'm going to be Sheila's daddy and give her everything she need. Listen, all you have to do is trust me. Follow my lead, do what I say, and you can't go wrong!"

Sasha was tired. She felt like she had been trying so hard on her own for so long and was getting nowhere. Everything Mark was saying sounded like the answer to all of her problems. "Ok, I choose you, and I trust you Mark."

"Finally, I got my dream girl. Now we about to take over the world!"

"Really, take over the world though Mark?"

"The whole world and everything in it baby. You'll see, sooner than you think. Now let's go in here and get this money…

***

"Mama, you look so good!" Denise greeted her mother with a big hug. She was completely overjoyed to see her. Nora had been in assisted living for almost a year now, recovering from the stroke she had. It was her day to be discharged and go home.

"Oh Denise, I'm so happy to be coming home! I honestly thought I would never get out of this place!" Nora began to weep. Her sister Veronica had been taking care of Denise and Sheila ever since Frank got arrested. Veronica consoled her sister with a hug.

"Nora we're all here for you! All you need to do is take things easy and get back to your old self!" Veronica was Nora's younger sister. They were very close and she always looked up to Nora.

"Veronica, I just want you to know that I really appreciate everything you've done for the girls! And I'm so glad the courts allowed you to be their temporary foster parent. I can never repay you for all that you've done sis."

"Ah don't start crying on me Nora, we're in this together! You know I love those girls as if they were my own! I'm not going to let anything happen to them or you."

"Has anybody gotten any recent news on Frank and his court hearing?" Nora hadn't spoken to Frank in months. She missed him terribly and wanted more than anything for her family to be back together.

"Well sis, they're really trying to give him a hard time, but he's a strong man! He has a hearing coming up in a few months. His attorney told me that the judge will decide then if he'll have to do a year in prison or get probation."

"I just really don't understand this! Frank was actually trying to correct our daughter. And they're just treating him like he's an animal!"

"Yeah, I don't feel like they're giving my brother in law a fair chance at all! And the system don't care about black families, you know how the law is. They see a good black man taking care of his family and what do they do? They take him away from the home as soon as they get an opportunity!"

"I don't know how I'm going to make it if he's not around! It's just too much to handle!"

"Ma it's going to be ok, you have us! And Sheila misses you a lot, she's getting so big!"

Nora's eyes instantly lit up at the thought of Sheila. "My little precious grandbaby, where is she?"

"She's at home with Eric (Veronica's son). It's so cold outside, and I hate to bring her out in this type of weather you know?"

"Yeah, you're right about that Veronica. I can't wait to see her! ... Well what about Sasha, how has she been? Is she keeping up with the job that Mrs. Gates set her up with?"

Denise and Veronica looked away, not wanting to respond. "Nora, that daughter of yours, I just don't know what in the hell has gotten into her!" Nora instantly felt distressed. "Now don't go getting yourself all worried and worked up over that girl Nora! You see what she's done already?! She's got you in the hospital and Frank put in jail! Sasha is nothing but trouble and you just need to not think about her! Remember she got caught selling drugs?! That's how Sheila got into foster care in the first place!"

Nora was overwhelmingly saddened. She always worried about Sasha and she just wanted to be there for her daughter. "Look Veronica, I know all of that ok! But that's still my daughter at the end of the day. And I'm responsible for her wellbeing!"

Her sister threw her hands up as to imply that she was done with the conversation. "Ok, that's the end of it then!! You're going to stay in the hospital if you keep worrying about that crazy ass girl! I'll be out in the car, just come out when you're ready to go!"...

"Mom, I know you love Sasha. I miss her like crazy too! But she is just really into a lifestyle that I can't even begin to understand!"

"What's been going on Denise? Please tell me, I need to know."

Denise really didn't want to stress her mother out with all of Sasha's crazy doings. But she knew her mother would just worry even more if she didn't know. "Well, do you remember Mark, Chauncey's best friend?"

Nora thought for a moment, trying to recollect who Mark was. "Yeah, yeah I remember him slightly. Chauncey brought him over to the house one time when we had that Fourth of July cookout last year."

"Exactly, that's him! Well Mama, he's been dating Sasha, and I guess they're living together now."

"What in the hell do you mean she's living with him?! How is my sixteen year old daughter living with a man?!"

"Yeah Mama, they've been together for about six months now. The worst part is that they're supposed to be moving to Miami in a week." Nora couldn't even wrap her mind around what Denise was saying. "Aunt Veronica tried to report Sasha as a runaway to the police multiple times. She'd come home for a day or two once they'd find her. But then she just goes back to Mark's house. The police won't even take the runaway reports anymore because they said Auntie knows where Sasha is already, so she's not considered a runaway. It's like we're damned if we do and damned if we don't! Auntie didn't want to tell you, but she gave up on the situation. She said her main concern right now is you, me, Sheila, and helping to get Dad out of jail. She thinks Sasha is a lost cause. And Ma to be honest, I hate to admit it but I think Auntie is right!"

Nora gave Denise a look that could cut like a knife. "Let me tell you something, that's your sister, you hear me?! And all y'all have is each other! You know I didn't raise you to be this way! You're supposed to be there for one another no matter what! Good or bad, what's wrong with you?!"

Denise was ashamed at what she had just said. "I know that Ma! It's just that you don't know everything we've been through, trying to get this girl to change! I will admit that she does give us money. But auntie won't take it because she said she knows its drug money. But I take it, just because I know we need the money."

Nora stood to her feet upon hearing this. "You better not take one more penny of that damn drug money! That's blood money and it's from the devil! And we don't eat with devils, do you understand?!"

"Yes Ma, loud and clear."

"Now you go outside with your aunt while I change clothes."

"Ok, do you want to get food or anything after we leave here?"

"No, I'm not in the mood to eat. You and your aunt are going to take me to see Sasha." …

***

"What do you think you're going to accomplish that I haven't already tried to?!" Veronica pleaded with her sister on the car ride to Mark's house.

"I'm looking to accomplish what any mother would in my predicament Veronica! I truly appreciate everything you've done with trying to get Sasha to come home, really I do. But I can't just leave it up to you. That's my daughter and at the end of the day I'm still responsible for her. We all know this situation is toxic and Sasha needs my help! I'm concerned for my daughter's life and safety! She's dating a well-known drug dealer and he's a gang member! And I'm sure the company he keeps is full of murderers that can harm my daughter at any moment! I won't have that happen to her!"

"Mom, you're just going to have to learn the hard way, you'll see. Sasha is not going to change, for you or anybody. She has to want to do that for herself. And just to let you know, she doesn't really look how she did the last time you saw her." …

It took about an hour to get to Mark's house. He lived outside the city in the suburbs. Nora was in amazement as she observed his neighborhood. Everyone drove brand new expensive foreign cars. The city was filled with large gated estates, lakes, ponds, and golf courses. "Now Frank would be in jail all over again if he knew how Sasha was living! I just can't believe this! Frank and I can't even afford homes like these after working for more than twenty years!"

They arrived at Mark's home. It was a beautiful two story brick colonial with French shutters. It looked like a home that belonged to a successful rich family. Not a teenage drug dealer from the inner city of Cleveland. They all got out of the car and walked up the marble pathway to the entrance of the front yard. Nora walked up the stairs first and proceeded to ring the doorbell. But before she got a chance to, she was met by Mark who was already opening the door.

"Mrs. Smith, how are you? Sasha didn't tell me we were having visitors today. Does she know you're here?"

"I don't need an invitation to see my daughter! That's my child and I'll see her anytime I damn well please!"

Mark gave Nora a stunned look. "Ok, obviously Sasha doesn't know you're here. Wait here while I go get her for you." He turned his back to Nora. But before shutting the door in her face, he mumbled something underneath his breath. "One week can't come fast enough. I can't wait until me and Sasha are out of here." Then he quickly shut the door.

"That boy really has some nerves!" Nora said as she turned away from the door.

"I told you honey, wasn't no sense in even coming here. This was a waste of time and gas!" Veronica complained as she walked away. "I'm going to wait in the car, this is too stressful of a situation for my nerves to bare! And I'm not trying to go to jail like Frank did!"...

"Well, here goes nothing." Nora said to Denise.

Suddenly, Sasha opened the door. "Mama?"

Nora looked at Sasha and instantly burst out into tears. "Sasha!" She grabbed her and hugged her tightly...

"Can we come in for a minute? Or do you think Mark will mind?"

"Of course y'all can Denise! Let's go in. Sasha took Nora by the hand and led her inside.

Nora observed the house as they entered. They walked through an atrium before even getting to the main entrance of the home. Expensive paintings hung on all the walls of each room. There were massive sized oriental rugs on the floors that looked custom made. And there was a beautiful black Baldwin piano in the living room. Clearly just there for decoration. It looked as if no one ever even played the thing. Above everything she saw, Sasha's appearance put Nora in shock the most. She was wearing high heeled shoes, a black leather mini skirt, and a silk red blouse that had a draping neck line. It exposed most of her cleavage. Nora could barely contain her thoughts and couldn't wait to say what was on her mind. Sasha seated them in the living room and Nora began to speak. She was deeply grieved by her daughter's lifestyle..."Sasha sweetheart, what are you doing with your life?! Have you gone completely crazy and out of your mind? I'm really having a hard time understanding all of this! It's like you have no regards at all to anything that's going on! Do you intentionally want to make matters worse than they already are?! And do you even care about your poor father and what he's going through right now?"

Sasha stood up and wiped the tears from her face. "Ma, of course I care about Daddy! Like seriously, why would you even ask me that?!"

"Because you're not acting like you give a damn about anybody except yourself! You don't even care about Sheila right now! And she's the person that matters the most!"

"You've got some nerves, coming into my house, and claiming that I don't care about my own daughter!"

Denise stood up and jumped into the conversation. She could see the maliciousness in her sister's eyes towards their mother. She reached out and grabbed Sasha's arm. "Just calm down ok, Mom is just trying to say that-"

Sasha pulled away furiously from Denise's grip. "Don't touch me! Everybody just get away from me!"

Denise was surprised and caught off guard. She didn't understand why her sister was so angry. "What did I do to you?!"

"Oh nothing at all, you're just being Denise. You always play the innocent roll!"

"Look Sasha, you're really out of line right now. Can you just calm down so we can talk about this?"

"Oh, so now you want to talk? What is there to talk about Denise? You only want to talk when Mom is around, or when I'm giving you money! Oh yea, and when you want me to keep your dirty ass little secrets! Well forget everything and everybody right now. I don't care about anything except for me and my daughter!"

Nora stood between the two of them, in fear that Sasha was about to physically attack Denise.

Mark overheard the commotion and entered the room. He came in and wrapped his arm around Sasha's waist. "Is everything ok baby, why is everybody yelling?"

"Boy, we don't need you coming in here, this is family business!"

"No Ma he is family! And he's the only one that really cares. Mark has been there for me and Sheila!"

Denise laughed sarcastically at the statement Sasha made.

"I don't think you can say too much Denise, you should just keep your mouth closed."

"Shut up Mark! You don't know me or anything about me so mind your own damn business!"

"You stay in your lane Mark, my daughter has nothing to do with this! Just who do you think you are, huh? You're just some thug out here in the streets that knows nothing about making an honest living. And you've got Sasha caught up in your schemes! You're a disgrace and so is your mother for allowing you to live this way!"

When Nora mentioned Mark's mother, he quickly removed his arm from Sasha's waist. Sensing his anger, Sasha grabbed his arm to stop him from approaching Nora.

"Baby, baby wait, come on now that's my mother!" Sasha pleaded with him.

"What, your mother? Fuck her! You want to talk about mothers? Sasha is the only real mother in this room!"

Sasha had both of her hands on his chest at this point, trying to get him to calm down. But he continued to lash out at Nora and Denise. "You think you've got everything under control Nora, well you don't! And that daughter of yours not so perfect!"

"Mark stop!" Sasha knew where he was trying to take the conversation and she begged him to leave the room.

"Yeah, you know the streets talk, and everybody knows about your daughter. Little Ms. Perfect, aka the baby killer."

Denise launched across the room, trying to attack Mark. But she was met by Sasha, and she pushed her away from him.

"Fuck you bitch!" Denise yelled at Mark.

"Fuck you too bitch!" Mark snapped back.

"Really though, who are you to say anything about me?! You sell drugs and kill people for a living, you sick bastard!"

He looked at Denise and gave her the most evil grin. Then he turned his attention to Nora. "What you saying about me, those are all rumors baby. But that Jamaican lady over on Harvard, you know the one that does those abortions in her basement? Word on the streets is that you went in to see her with a situation, and when you left your situation was gone. The streets talk baby."

Denise ran out of the house crying hysterically.

Sasha slumped down onto the couch. She was completely shocked at her man and the vicious verbal attack he made on her sister. "Mark why would you say that to her?!"

"Look Sasha, we need to finish packing. Finish up in here so we can do what needs to get done!" He disregarded everything she said and focused his attention back on Nora. She had a look of devastation all over her face. Finally, Mark left the room.

Nora walked over to Sasha and slapped her across the face. Sasha was so furious that she had to control herself and not retaliate on her mother.

"I think it's time for you to leave Ma!" Sasha was struggling to hold back her tears of anger and hurt towards her mother.

"Leave and do what?! Leave and take care of your daughter Sasha?! You let this man humiliate me, your sister, and -"

"Ma he didn't humiliate anyone, Denise humiliated herself! I wasn't going to tell you about the abortion and I had no idea that Mark would do that!"

"You lying bitch!"

Sasha was shocked. Her mother never cursed at her, so she knew she must have been really upset. "You act like I haven't tried to get back custody of Sheila Ma!"

"Oh you did, well what happened with that Sasha?!"

"Ma, they're really giving me a hard time! Mrs. Gates is such a bitch, and she's really making it difficult for me to show proof of residency and employment. You know, to show that I can financially support Sheila. Mama Mark has a legit auto body business, and -"

"Just stop it Sasha, I don't want to hear another word about it!!"

"Mama, maybe Sheila being with you all right now is the best thing, until I can get on my feet a little more."

Nora laughed at her comment.

"What's funny?" Sasha asked, as if confused.

"Child, you're already living in this nice neighborhood! You have a beautiful home, and you're telling me that's not being on your feet? What more do you need, a damn spaceship?! You will never be what you need to be for your daughter. You just simply don't care!"

"Ok, I'm not taking any more verbal assaults from you Ma! I was going to wait to tell you, but next week, Mark and I are moving to Miami."

"Moving to Miami?! And just who is going to take care of Sheila? Sasha I hope you don't think that you can just run away from your responsibilities like this! You have a one year old daughter for God's sake girl!"

"I know, that's exactly why I need to make this move Ma! Mark's family is opening up a restaurant down there and they need all the help they can get! And it's a great opportunity for me to build something for Sheila! I'm telling you, we've got it all planned out Ma!"

Nora grabbed her jacket and clinched it tightly in her hand. "You're aunt told me on the way here that this was just a waste of time. And she told me that you'd just cause me to be right back in the hospital. You know what, she was right!"

Sasha walked away from her mother and began pacing the floor. "Fine Ma, believe everything that everybody says about me! It's nice to know that my own mother doesn't even believe in me!"

Nora approached Sasha face to face. "Your family are the only ones who care about you! These low lives you're hanging with, believe me, they don't give a damn about you or your child's life!

Your aunt has been there taking care of your baby along with your sister! Not you or this thug that you're with! So don't you give me this bull shit about who doesn't care! Sasha, I never thought in all the days of my life that you would turn out like this! Your father and I have always struggled to give you and your sister the best we could afford! We may not be rich, but we have morals and values. Clearly you lost sight of all that! I have no choice but to let you go, since you've already made your decision! Nora turned away from Sasha and began walking towards the door. Sasha frantically followed behind her in an attempt to say something to try and mend things with her mother.

"Ma wait, please wait!" They stopped in the atrium. Nora stared at Sasha with eyes full of pain.

Sasha could barely stand to look at her mother. "Ma, I'm so sorry for everything! I never meant to hurt anyone, and I'm sorry I'm not the daughter you wanted me to be! "I'm just so caught up in this lifestyle right now, and I don't know how to get out of it! I need help Ma!"

"Sasha, I've done all that I can do for you as of this point. And quite frankly, there is nothing else I can do. You have to want a better life for you and your daughter! But I will promise you one thing, I'll raise Sheila to be a respectful woman with morals. And when you're ready to be in her life, you're more than welcome. We would never try to keep you away from your child. But we would need to know for sure that you have a safe and proper environment for her. That is if you decide to ever come back."

"I'm coming back for my baby Ma, I promise!"

Nora forced a smile while looking at her daughter. Then she took the back of her hand and caressed Sasha's face in a gentle manner. Like a mother would do to her young child. "Sure you will Sasha." Then she turned away and walked out the door. Sasha watched her mother walk away from her until she was out of sight. Little did Sasha know, she wouldn't see her family or Sheila for the next ten years…

Sheila's story

"By now I'm sure you can tell that I didn't get a fair start in life. I was born to a fifteen year old teenager that didn't have a clue about how to be a mother. My father was a major drug dealer, and I didn't really know him until I was eleven years old. Life really throws you all types of curve balls. If it wasn't for my grandparents, I don't know where I'd be right now. And it hasn't been easy at all! Going through school and seeing all of your friends grow up with both of their parents at home. Whenever I was asked about my parents I had to pretend like they were around. Truth is my mother is a recovering crack addict and my father sells it. Yeah, the cards definitely weren't dealt in my favor, but I vowed to never be like either one of my parents. In some crazy way I don't even look at them as parents. Shit, I feel like my mother never wanted me from birth anyway. She abandoned me and ran away from home shortly after I was born! Thank God for my grandparents! My grandpa showed me what a real man looks like and how he's supposed to take care of his family. And my grandma showed me how to be a woman. She always told me not to open my legs for any and every man out here.

Now that I'm seventeen, I've just been really thinking about what I want to do with my life. Trying to figure out where I want to go and what I want to be. All I know for sure is that I don't want to be like my mother or my father."...Sheila was talking to her co-worker at work while on a lunch break.

"Girl that's crazy as fuck! Honestly, you were dealt a bad hand in life. I don't know many people that could remain so positive about it. I know I couldn't!"

"What can you really do about it Chivon? All you can do is take it as a lesson learned and keep it moving right?"

"Yeah, I guess so... But girl on a lighter note, I'm so excited about senior prom, I can't wait! I've got my colors picked out and everything! My dress is going to be a powder pink color. And my boyfriend is going to wear a cream colored tuxedo with the powder pink gator shoes and shirt to match! All eyes will definitely be on us! And everybody will have something to say as they all stop and stare. Anyway, who are you going to prom with Sheila? You never told me."

"Well you know Ryan and I started dating, and girl he's finally giving us a title. So hopefully everything goes as planned so that we can have a good time at prom, you know?"

"Girl I know! I can tell that you really like him too! Y'all been dating for a while now right?"

"Yeah, we've been together for about a year now. I just really hate his lifestyle and what he does!"

"What type of lifestyle is he living?"

"Girl you know, he's in the game. But he only sells weed. I just wish he would do something legit! He's so smart and he really doesn't have to do what he does! But of course he loves the fast money. His uncle owns the Millennium nightclub downtown, and Ryan could practically run the place! But he claims that's slow money! I'm like really dude, $5k a month is slow money?! I just don't want him to go to jail! He's already been locked up in Juvenile, and now that he's eighteen any serious charges would land him in prison."

"Yes honey, he definitely needs to slow his ass down! So Sheila, have y'all had sex yet?"

"Hell nah we haven't had sex!"

"Oh ok my bad girl! I just thought you might have been giving him some of that sweet cookie because of how close ya'll are!"

Sheila shook her head in disagreement. "Girl, ain't nobody had a piece of my cookie, I'm still a virgin."

"A virgin, girl do those still even exist anymore?!"

Sheila didn't understand why Chivon was so surprised at her being a virgin. "Yes girl a virgin and they do still exist!"

"Yeah they do, if you're like eleven or twelve years old! Shit, girl I lost my virginity when I was thirteen and I've been fucking ever since! You know you're going to have a lot to learn when you finally do have sex! I mean damn, you aint even been broken in yet! Your first dick is going to hurt like hell!"

The girls started laughing.

"But seriously though, what are you doing, waiting to get married or some shit like that? Sheila nobody is a virgin when they get married nowadays! Plus you need the experience so you can know what you like! You need to be able to know good sex from bad sex."

"Chivon girl pump your brakes! You make sex sound like I'm going shopping for a damn car! Besides, I don't want to take too many test drives and put all those miles on my ride, you feel me?" The girls high five one another.

"You right about that Sheila! I got a few that I wish never came close to this pussy, let alone hit it!"

"Damn girl, see that's what I'm afraid of going through!"

"Don't worry, you'll know when it's the right time and the right person Sheila."

"Yeah, I hope so." Sheila looked down at her watch, she didn't realize they were ten minutes late past their break time. She stood up frantically.

"What's wrong, is everything ok?!"

"Girl we're late from break, we need to get back to work!"

"Oh shit!" They both hurried to collect their things and rushed back to work...

***

It was time for Sheila to get off from work. She made plans to meet up with Ryan and have him pick her up. After clocking out, she went outside and sat on a nearby bench waiting for him to arrive. Ryan was Sheila's first real boyfriend, and she really liked him a lot. He was a scrawny guy. He stood about 6'1", with tattoos and a low cut fade. He wasn't the most handsome guy on the block but he was very popular and he had a great personality. Everyone knew him in the city from being a drug dealer. He really made Sheila feel special and he always told her what she wanted to hear. His family loved her as well and Sheila really thought she had a future with him. Finally, he pulled up in his 2003 Jeep Cherokee and Sheila got in.

"Hey boo," Ryan said as he kissed her on the cheek. She was always so excited to see him, and the smell of his cologne intrigued her every time. "How was your day?"

"It was good. I couldn't wait to get off so that I could see you though."

"Ah look at you, trying to be all sweet and shit."

Sheila laughed, Ryan was quite the comedian and he always kept her smiling. It was one of the main things that attracted her to him…

He decided to take her to the lake. There was a trail that allowed them to walk around the lakefront and watch the sunset. It was a popular hangout spot in the city and it was ideal for a romantic date. "So, what we doing about this prom shit, you figured out what we wearing Sheila?"

"Yeah, I've been thinking about it a lot, you know, like what colors I want to wear and all of that."

"Oh that's simple boo, we wearing red. You know I rep my bleeds wherever I go." Ryan was a part of the Bloods, but he kept his circle of friends very small. He always stayed to himself, and never really hung with a large group of people.

"Ryan, I thought we talked about this! You said you were going to stop all of this gang banging shit! I thought you wanted to go back to school so that you could graduate! You should really consider working at your uncle's club, I think it would be a good fit for you baby!"

"See Sheila, that's why I like you. You always try to see the good in a nigga, even when he can't see it in himself. I don't know if that school shit is really for me though. I mean the work easy as fuck, I'm a smart dude. I'm just not go use none of that shit in my everyday life! Now what I could do is network with those college kids that got rich parents. That way I could build up my clientele for this drug shit. But seriously Sheila, a nigga like me don't know what to do with his life. You know what I'm saying? I know I'm good at selling drugs. I'm a street nigga and I like moving shit and making things happen. If the streets want it, I got the best of it and I stay moving it. Can't no other nigga hustle better than me, my drive too strong for them baby. These other niggas weak out here!"

As Sheila sat and listened to Ryan, she imagined what he would be like if he changed his mind-set into doing positive things. He possessed all the qualities of an entrepreneur. Only if he could channel his skills into doing something legal... "We have to figure this thing out Ryan. I love you so much, and I can't see myself being with anybody except you. I'm concerned about your life style and I don't want to see you get into any more trouble baby."...

After their date at the lake, Ryan and Sheila arrived back at her house. "Sheila, you really make me want to think about doing something different with my life. I never thought about wanting to be a better man, but you changed that."

Sheila could barely contain herself, it was everything she ever wanted to hear him say. "Baby you can do anything you put your mind to! Look, it's the beginning of senior year, so we have the entire school year to figure things out. All we need to do is come up with a really good plan!"

"I know Sheila. I just need to stay focused on getting out of this drug game. You might not believe me, but a nigga don't want to do this shit forever. I'm constantly watching my back, worrying if a nigga trying to rob me, or even worse kill me. People call me all hours of the day and night for weed and dope. I hustle both of them you know."

"No, I didn't know that!" Sheila was upset at hearing this because she knew what type of customers came with selling dope. Most crack heads would steal from their own mother. And she wanted Ryan to have no dealings with those sorts of people. "Ryan you have to stop this now!"

He looked at Sheila and laughed.

"What's so funny?"

"You and your little imagination. Sometimes I think you live in a box baby. It doesn't work that easy out here in the streets. When you take oaths, you ride that shit out, even if it's to the death of you."

Sheila's heart sank, she almost felt like she never knew this side of him. It scared her, but curiosity made her attracted at the same time. "I just don't know what to think about all of this Ryan."

"You don't have to think about any of it. Me and you good baby, that's all that matters. As long as I'm with you, and I'm not causing you any drama, then you don't have anything to worry about." Ryan's cell phone began to go off in the midst of their conversation. He looked down to read a text message... *I need an eighth of that good shit, is you still coming?* "Damn!" Ryan scrambled to look for his keys and start up his car. He forgot all about the lick he was supposed to hit. And he hated missing out on any money.

"What's wrong baby, who was that?"

"I forgot to get my mom something from the store for dinner tonight, I need to go."

"Oh ok, well Ryan before you go, I just want to tell you something."

"Ok, what's up boo?"

"I've been thinking a lot about something lately, like sex."

"You been thinking about sex, for what?!"

"Yes silly," Sheila giggled at his reaction.

"Sheila, don't you think your first time should be special, like with someone you'll marry?"

"So what, you don't want to marry me one day?!"

"I didn't say that, I'm just saying we in a good place right now, and I think we shouldn't rush into things. The last thing I want to do is hurt you."

Sheila threw herself back into her seat and folded her arms. "Oh, so now you'll hurt me? I knew this was too good to be true with you! I mean come on dude, you're not a virgin, and you've been with multiple girls! So how are you even holding out without having sex?!"

"Really, are we actually having this conversation right now Sheila? Don't compare me to these niggas out here that's thirsty for some ass. Yeah, I have fucked a lot of hoes, and it doesn't mean shit because I'm not with them! And no real nigga wants a bitch that just throws him the pussy without a chase. You not easy and I respect you for that. I treat a hoe like a hoe and I just fuck her. But I treat you different, I got plans for us. I'll probably fuck around and fall in love with that pussy girl. You just want a nigga sprung out here! See how you plotting on me?!"

Sheila couldn't stop laughing. She leaned over, put her arms around his neck, and kissed him. "Ryan, you are so special to me. I want my first time to be with someone I'd be with forever, and that's you!"

Ryan kissed Sheila's for head. "Everything that's meant to happen will happen, ok? Believe me, I want you just as bad. I just need to make sure I'm everything you need me to be for you. Now let me get out of here and make this run for mom dukes, and I'll call you later. Plus I don't want your grandparents pulling up on us. You know your grandfather don't like gang banging niggas."

"He could like you if he got to know the Ryan that I know."...

***

"Sheila its time to get up, you overslept again!" Nora yelled out to Sheila from downstairs. It was time for her to go to school.

"Ok Ma!" She got dressed and headed downstairs for breakfast.

"Hey, how are you feeling this morning?"

"I feel ok Ma, there's just a lot on my mind."

"Now what could a seventeen-year old teenager have to think about besides what to eat and what to wear?"

"I wish it were that simple! I've got the SAT and ACT tests coming up, and you know I'm not a good test taker. I still haven't figured out which college I want to go to. And I need a better job because I need at least a thousand dollars for prom! Ugh, it's just too much going on and I can't handle it all at once!"

Nora took a seat at the table with Sheila. "Sweetie, all of those things you're worrying about are exactly what you just said, THINGS you're worried about. Don't let these small THINGS control your life, because life is more important than that! And you're a great test taker! With a little bit of hard work and studying you'll do just fine. God will protect you and give you all the strength and knowledge that you need."

Nora hugged Sheila and kissed her on the cheek. She always raised her to be a proud and respectable black woman with morals and integrity. Sheila had been nominated for multiple awards throughout her community and school over the years. She was always an honor roll student, and she was well behaved. Nora and Frank loved her dearly. And they raised her as if she were their own daughter.

"And by the way, Sasha called you the other day. She wanted to speak to you but you weren't here. I told her you were at work"

As far as Sheila was concerned, she had no relationship with her mother. There were only a handful of moments she could recall spending with Sasha. "Well Ma you're my mother, and you're the only mother that I need."

"Now you look here, Frank and I have helped to raise you, but I'm not your mother! You only have one mother and you need to respect her, regardless of how you feel! She may not be doing everything right, but she's still your mother! And you only get one mother in this life so you better cherish her!"

Nora never liked the ill feelings that Sheila had towards Sasha. Her view on things were that Sasha was young when she had Sheila. And she felt like Sasha could have never been a real mother to her because of that… "Your mother is trying to do the best she can and you know that! It hasn't been easy for her, being in and out of rehab, and moving from state to state. Give the girl some credit for even trying to have a relationship with you!"

"Yeah, well she never came back for me, so it's like she never really wanted me anyway!"

"Well Sheila she said she had something to tell us all but she wanted you to be around when she shared the good news."

Frank came downstairs at that point and joined Sheila and Nora in the kitchen. "Good morning, how are my beautiful ladies doing?"

"Just fine, I was telling Sheila that Sasha called the other day and said that she had some good news for everyone."

"Oh yeah? Well you just make sure I'm not around when she wants to share this good news. I want nothing to do with her and I don't want to hear anything she has to say." Frank and Sasha hadn't spoken since he came home from jail over fifteen years ago. He basically disowned her, claiming that he wanted nothing to do with her ever again. "Damn Nora, everything goes good until you start talking about Sasha! And I know Sheila doesn't want to hear about her either!"

"You two have a lot of nerves! For God's sake, that's your daughter Frank! She didn't deliberately do anything to you! You're mad about something that happened over fifteen years ago! Get over it, life is too short! We can all have a new beginning if you two would just open up and give her a chance!"

"Well I'm sorry baby, but I ran out of chances with that girl a long time ago! And what did she do? She had a baby at fifteen, got me sent to jail for one year, and put you in the hospital for over six months! And you just want everything to go back to normal!? Not in this lifetime baby!" Frank grabbed his cup of coffee and his jacket. "Alright I'm going to work. I'll talk to you two later."

"Bye Daddy... See Mama, why you have to get everybody all upset like that?"

"I'm done with it!" Nora replied as she went upstairs.

Sheila turned her attention to the television as she ate her breakfast. Suddenly, there was a knock at the door...

"Hey girl, you ready to go?" It was her friend Deborah that lived across the street. She always rode to school with Sheila in the mornings. They had been friends since the seventh grade. And they hung out all of the time.

"Yeah in a minute, just let me finish eating. Come in and wait until I'm done."...

"So what's up?"

"Nothing much girl. I'm so ready to get this school day over with already."

"I know that's right! Don't you have a track meet today?"

"Yeah I do, and you better come Sheila!"

"Damn, I have to go to work today, or else you know I would be there girl!"

"Um hmm, sure you would. So how you and your boo doing?"

"Oh we're good. I was just with him last night when I got off work. I really think I want him to be the one Deborah."

"You want him to be the one for what?"

"I want him to be the one to take my virginity girl!"

"Take your virginity!" Deborah blurted out.

"Girl you better lower your damn voice! You want my grandmother to come down here and have a heart attack?!"

"Damn girl my bad!

"Let's get to school before we're late Deborah."...

***

It was the end of the school day and Frank had arrived to pick up Sheila. "So how was your day?"

"Oh it was just great! Trigonometry, History, English, you've got to love that stuff." Sheila said sarcastically.

"Yeah, well while you're making jokes, I hope you've been seriously thinking about what you're going to do with your life after high school. Instead of dating that knuckle head boy Bryan."

"Daddy, his name is Ryan!"

"Bryan, Ryan, or whatever the hell his name is! I don't approve of you and him at all! He's no good for you and as far as I'm concerned he doesn't want anything out of life. Every time I've seen that fool he's got his pants hanging off his ass, and a red bandanna wrapped around his head! He must be one of those gang members. You'll end up just like your mother and I'll cut you off just like I did her."

Sheila slumped down in her seat and sighed. "Daddy, Ryan is a great guy if you would just get to know him!"

"Let me tell you something. I'm a grown ass man, and aint no teenager going to tell me what I need to do. Besides, I've seen all I need to see from him." Frank pulled into the parking lot of Sheila's job. "I don't want you working too many hours. You're still in school and you need time to study. What time are you getting off tonight anyway?"

"Daddy, you know I'm not going to be your little girl forever right? And I'm only working four hours today." She reached over to kiss him on the cheek.

"Rather you like it or not, you'll always be my little girl. Do you need me to pick you up from work later?"

Sheila thought quickly to come up with a lie, knowing that Ryan always picked her up from work. No that's ok, my co-worker is going to give me a ride home."

***

It was almost the end of Sheila's work shift when Chivon walked over to her register. "Girl wait until I tell you this!"

"Oh goodness, what happened now, is it you and Mike?" Sheila thought Chivon had some wild and crazy relationship story to tell.

"No, just take a quick break after you ring out this customer!"

"Ok," When Sheila got done with her customer, she walked outside of the store to meet Chivon. "So what's up, what do you want now?"

"It's not what I want Miss Thang! You see that fine light skinned dude over there with the brown eyes?"

Sheila looked across the street. There was a guy sitting on the hood of his car. It was a 1989 chocolate colored Buick cutlass, and it was a beauty. Shining rims with the t top hood, it was definitely a classic. While he was staring at her from across the street, Sheila recognized him instantly. She'd seen him come into the store a few times before.

"Girl, what in the hell is going on?! Why did you bring me out here to stare at a man across the street, I'm with Ryan!"

"Sheila, you need to keep your options open! This guy is friends with my older brother Phil. He just saw me in the store while I was clocking out, and he asked me how Phil was doing. When we were done talking, I told him I was about to go holler at you before I leave. Girl, right away he started saying how he always comes into the store just to see you! Then he said he wanted to meet you!"

Sheila was extremely taken back. A part of her was flattered for even thinking this guy liked her. He didn't seem like he'd be interested in a girl like her. She just considered herself as a regular chick from around the way. "Chivon, I'm about to go back to work, I don't have time for this." But before Sheila could turn around to go back inside, the guy had already crossed the street and was approaching her.

Once face to face with her, he extended his hand in an attempt to shake hers. "Hey beautiful"...

Now Sheila remembered him being handsome, but up close he was mesmerizing. "Hello," Sheila replied in a low and meek tone.

"Well, my work here is done!" Chivon said as she walked off.

"That girl is crazy."

"Yeah, that's my homeboy's little sister, she's always been the life of the party."

They both laugh. Sheila found herself instantly attracted to this guy. Just hearing his voice made her imagination run wild. She quickly collected her thoughts and cleared her throat. "Look, it was really nice meeting you, but I have to get back to work. Chivon told me that you -"

"My name is Lawrence, what's yours?" He caught her off guard by abruptly interrupting her. "Well, my name is Sheila. And as I was saying, it was nice meeting you but I have to get back to work."

"I understand Ms. Sheila. And by the way, Sheila is a pretty name. A pretty name for a beautiful girl."

Sheila started to blush. "Well thanks, that's really sweet of you, Lawrence right?"

"Yes, Lawrence sweetheart."

He seemed like such a gentlemen. Sheila wasn't use to a guy talking so sweet to her. Not that Ryan didn't, it just seemed different and refreshing.

"So can I call you sometimes Sheila? I would love to get to know you."

"Well I have a boyfriend, so that might not be a good idea."

Lawrence smiled and briefly looked away while licking his lips. Sheila almost melted at the sight. And naughty thoughts began to invade her mind.

"No offense, but I didn't ask you if you had a boyfriend. I asked you if I could get to know you. I'm not trying to disrespect your relationship. I just want to have a conversation, that's all."

Sheila thought about it for a second. "Well, I guess there's nothing wrong with that."

He pulled out his cell phone to take her number. Then he took her hand and kissed the back of it. "It was a pleasure meeting you, and I can't wait to talk to you soon beautiful."…

***

It was the end of Sheila's work shift. She went outside as usual to sit on the bench, waiting for Ryan to pick her up. Fifteen minutes went by, and he still hadn't shown up. Sheila called his cell phone numerous times, but it kept going straight to the voicemail. She began to get worried. *This isn't like him, why is his phone off and why hasn't he gotten here by now?* She thought to herself.

About ten minutes later, a car pulled up and stopped right in front of her. It was Ryan's younger brother Darwin. He quickly got out of the car and approached her with a look of worry all over his face. "Sheila, I got here as quick as I could!"

"Darwin what's wrong, what are you doing here?!"

"Everything just went all bad Sheila! Ryan had a drug deal that went wrong. He served some dude that turned out to be an undercover cop, and he got arrested!"

"What, how did you find out about this?!"

"He called me earlier from jail, and he told me you'd be waiting on him! He wanted me to pick you up and tell you everything that's going on. Right now our entire family is meeting up at my mother's house so we can come up with a plan to get my brother out of jail."…

The build up

Darwin and Sheila arrived at his mother's house. He turned off the ignition and looked over at her. From the look on his face, you could tell that he was full of distress. Probably wondering what his brother could have possibly gotten himself into this time... "I don't know when this nigga is going to change his life! I mean damn, we just got home from doing a bid! I'm tired of getting caught up with him and his schemes!"

    Darwin was referring to the theft case he got caught in with Ryan a few years ago. They were both sentenced to two years in Juvenile Jail because they were riding around in a stolen car with guns and drugs. Darwin was the driver while Ryan decided to commit a robbery. He ended up getting sentenced to twenty four months just because he was in the car with Ryan. The police didn't believe his story about not knowing the car was stolen or that there were guns and drugs inside. But Darwin really was telling the truth. "He's not only destroying his life, but everyone else's life around him! Friends, family, it doesn't matter! He's selfish as fuck!" Darwin slumped over his steering wheel and covered his head with his arms.

    Sheila felt so bad for him. She understood why he was angry about getting sentenced because of Ryan. But she never knew how much resentment he had towards his brother. She placed her arm around his shoulders, trying to console him. "Look Darwin, I can only begin to imagine how you must feel. You already lost two years of your life due to something that your brother put you up to. But let's not jump to conclusions as far as this situation is concerned. We don't even know all the details right? And I'm sure Ryan feels terrible about what happened between the two of you! I know he loves you Darwin because he talks about you all the time! Let's just go inside and see if we can find out any new information, ok?"

He lifted his head and stared Sheila directly in the eyes. "You're a good girl Sheila. How did you end up with a nigga like my brother?" He didn't wait for her to respond. Instead he opened his door and got out of the car. Sheila didn't know how to react to what he just said. So she dismissed the comment and followed him inside the house...

***

Sheila didn't get home until after midnight. She knew her grandparents would kill her if they knew she had just gotten in. Her shift ended over three hours ago and she was supposed to be home no later than 10 p.m. As she walked to the door to put her key in, she was met by her grandfather who vigorously opened the door for her. Then he grabbed her by the arm and yanked her inside.

"Where in the hell have you been?!" He looked furious and had clearly been waiting for Sheila to get home. "And who was that boy that dropped you off?!"

Nora came downstairs at this point, joining Sheila and Frank. "Frank close the door, the neighbors are going to hear everything!" He slammed the door shut and pulled Sheila into the living room.

"Sheila, you know you were supposed to be home hours ago! You had us worried sick about you! We are too old to be up waiting around and worrying like this!"

"Ma, I can explain. I was supposed to get a ride home from Ryan, but -"

"Wait, what do you mean you were supposed to get a ride home from Ryan?! I thought you told Frank that your co-worker was dropping you off? So you lied to us?!"

Sheila was flustered and afraid of saying the wrong thing. "I did lie, and I'm so sorry!" Sheila looked down in shame. Meanwhile Frank was outraged.

"You're just like your mother. A good for nothing ass child! I can't trust you, you lying ass -"

"Frank stop it!" Nora interrupted and quickly stood between the two of them. "We're not doing this! Not tonight, and not this way! History will not repeat itself! Frank, just go upstairs for a moment and calm down before you say something that you'll regret!" Nora shoved him on the chest, as to motion him towards the stairway. He turned away and went upstairs. Nora took Sheila by the forearm and led her into the kitchen. "Sheila where were you, and why did you lie to us?!"

"Ma, I know it was wrong to lie. But Daddy already doesn't like Ryan, so what was I supposed to do?"

"You were supposed to tell us the truth Sheila! Don't you know that we have your best interests at hand? Honey we know you better than you know yourself! Ryan is a bad influence on you, and he doesn't want any type of decent life for himself!"

Sheila shook her head in disagreement. "No Mama, no! You don't know what you're saying! He's a good guy! Y'all don't know him like I do!"

"You're still a young girl Sheila. You have a long way to go and a lot of living to do! You can't possibly know what's good for you right now! If you did, you'd know that dealing with a guy like Ryan is a liability to you! You have a lot to offer any man, and you have so much going for yourself! Any fool can see that baby! But you've got to make sure you're not entertaining those fools honey! They'll take advantage of you. And Mama hates to be the one to tell you this, but Ryan is one of those fools that you're entertaining!"

Sheila began to cry even harder. Somehow what her grandmother said had hit her like a ton of bricks. Somewhere deep down inside, she knew Nora was right. "Well, I'm sure you and Daddy will be happy to know that I won't be seeing Ryan for a very long time."

"And why is that?"

"I was at his mother's house. His brother came to pick me up from work. Ryan called him from jail and said that he had gotten arrested."

"Oh my, now do you see what I mean?! This is exactly what I was talking about. He's no good for you!"

"Ma he just made a bad choice, everyone does that! He has the potential to be a good man!"

"Yeah, well you can't go around in life looking at someone's potential, because it's not reality! So what happened, why is he in jail?"

Sheila wasn't going to tell her grandmother what really happened. She found out that Ryan was facing three to four years in prison. This would just convince her grandparents even more that he was no good for her. She tried to brainstorm quickly and come up with a lie.

"Well, he just had some prior things going on with traffic tickets that built up. So he has to sit in jail for a while until it's taken care of, nothing too serious."

"Well whatever the reason is, from this day forward you will have nothing to do with him!"

Sheila didn't even try to contend with her grandmother's demand. At this point, she knew they would never understand how she felt about him. "Ok Ma, I'll never talk to him again."

"It's late, so we'll talk about this more in the morning. That way everyone is cooled down and can talk reasonably. Your grandfather and I will discuss you're punishment as well."

Sheila went upstairs to her room, buried her head in her pillow, and cried miserably for the rest of the night...

***

It was the next morning, and Sheila was drained. She had been up all night crying and all she could think about was Ryan. *How long would he be gone? How would she talk to him?* And on top of all that, now she didn't have a date for the senior prom.

"Sheila, can you tell us what the sum of X is in this equation?" It was 3rd period in Mrs. Fredrick's Math class, and Sheila wasn't even paying attention to begin with.

"Um, I think, its-" Sheila scrambled for an answer.

"Wouldn't the answer be sixteen Mrs. Fredrick?" Sheila's best friend Lashonda was sitting next to her, so she blurted out the answer in her defense.

"Actually it would be 24. And Lashonda, I didn't ask you for the answer. The question was clearly directed at Sheila."

"Oh, I'm sorry Mrs. Fredrick, I didn't hear that part! I thought it was an open question for the class!"...

Saved by the bell, Sheila thought to herself as the school bell rang.

"Ok class, tomorrow I need you to have your group projects turned in on time! If it's late it'll be a permanent zero! Have a good day!"...

Sheila and Lashonda headed towards the door and out into the hallway. Deborah followed behind to catch up with them.

"Girl, thanks for saving my ass! I know you can tell I've been going through it all night right?!"

"Honey, you look like you've been going through it all night and now it's going to be all day!"

Deborah chimed in on the conversation as she approached the two. "Don't worry about it girl, I understand. It's hard to stay focused in Mrs. Fredrick's class just on a regular day!" Deborah joked, the girls laugh.

"I don't know what I'm going to do, my heart is broken! I find a man that I'm in love with, and now he's gone!"

"It'll be ok! You're expecting the worse to happen. Ryan's case may not even be that serious!"

Lashonda and Sheila both looked at Deborah in disagreement. "No sweetie, it's definitely that serious!"

"Damn, why you got to be so negative Lashonda! Can't you see that Sheila is already worried about it enough?"

"It's ok Deborah, she's right. Ryan's probation officer already warned him that if he got into more trouble within the next two years, he could face at least two years in prison. This is what I'm having a hard time understanding! We just talked about this the other night! He knew what he was supposed to do to stay out of trouble! And he goes and does this?! It's just stupid and irresponsible on his part!"

"Damn! So will he get a bond posted or anything?" Deborah asked.

"Well, I was at his mom's house last night. And his lawyer told her that his bond is fucking $50k! He needs at least ten percent of that to even post bond! No one has that type of money! Not his mother and of course not me! The money he did have saved up was seized during a drug raid. Ryan had this undercover drug house that I didn't even know about! He kept so many secrets from me. I feel hurt, lost, and betrayed!"

"Girl it's going to be ok!" Lashonda insisted.

"Yeah, you know we got your back, we're in this together." Deborah added.

"Y'all are my true friends for life!" The girls all gave each other a hug. "I have to go to Chemistry class, but I need a favor from one of you."

"Sure, what's up Sheila?"

"Well Lashonda, you know my grandparents don't like Ryan. And I couldn't dare tell them the real reason why he got locked up! They already grounded me for a month! If they knew the truth I'd be grounded for life or end up dead at the hands of my grandfather."

"So what do you need us to do?" Deborah asked.

"Well, I want to write him a letter. And since I can't get his letters delivered to my house, I was wondering if he could send letters for me to one of y'all houses?"

"That might be a problem for me. Any mail addressed from prison is going to break all hell loose in my household!" The girls laughed. Lashonda's parents were divorced, and her father remarried a female Pastor who was extremely strict and religious.

"You can just have him send the letters to my house, my parents won't mind."

"Thank you so much Deborah, I owe you one girl!"...

Daddy home

School was over for the day, and Sheila had the day off from work. She went home to take a quick nap, but before she could, there was a knock at the door. She looked through the peep hole to see who was at the door. It was her father. Sheila hadn't seen him in over a year. She opened the door…"Yo, I figured you'd be home by now, where Frank and Nora at?" Chauncey didn't come into Sheila's life consistently until she was eleven years old. He approached her one day while she was outside playing, and began to ask her all sorts of questions. Like if she knew who her father was, or where he was, instead of just introducing himself as her dad. Before that she had only seen him a handful of times when she was six or seven. She remembered one moment especially when Sasha took her to visit him. He picked her up, held her in the air, and playfully acted as if he was going to throw her into this huge black trash can. The bad part about it was that Sheila felt like her parents threw her away in real life. Her father was right in front of her asking all of these questions and she didn't even recognize him. Once he left that day, Sheila ran into the house to tell Nora what happened. Nora in return told Sasha, and she knew right away that it was Chauncey trying to come back into Sheila's life. And sure enough it was. From that moment on, he came around more often. But Sheila felt like he always played mind games with her.

"Hey, I wasn't expecting to see you."

"Well it would be nice if you invited me in for a minute instead of treating me like a Jehovah's Witness at the door!" Sheila led him inside. "Yo, you don't look too happy to see me?"

"No, it's not that. I just wasn't expecting you." Sheila looked off, not wanting to make eye contact with her father. "So how long have you been in town?" Chauncey stayed in Philly, but he would travel back and forth from Philadelphia to Cleveland to visit his mother. She lived three blocks over from Nora. Sheila only met her grandmother a few times. And it seemed like she never really showed Sheila any type of affection. She always gave off a weird vibe. Almost as if not wanting to get too close. Maybe she had doubts about Sheila being Chauncey's daughter. Back in the day, there was a rumor floating around that a man named Beano was Sheila's father. When Sheila was born she came out looking all bright and light-skinned, just like Beano. Although Sasha and Beano use to date, Chauncey knew that this wasn't the case. He took Sasha's virginity and was the only man she had ever been with intimately at the time.

"I'm up here visiting your grandmother. She hasn't been feeling very well lately. You should go by and see her more often."

"Yeah, I definitely have to stop by more often." In her mind, Sheila was thinking that would be a lot easier said than done. She only had two people she felt comfortable with on Chauncey's side of the family. Her cousin Briana, and her brother Cartier.

"Look, you've been on my mind a lot lately. Not a day goes by that I don't think about you. You're my daughter and my first born. You are the most important woman in my life and I would never put any other woman before you. You and I haven't had the best relationship, and you don't get to see me that often. But you know how my lifestyle is. I'm always on the move yo, trying to establish something big so we can all be stable and not want for nothing."

Sheila thought about what her father was saying. She always had ill feelings towards him for not being around like he should have been. But to hear him say she was the most important woman in his life made her feel like he put her on a pedestal that no one could ever take her off of. She longed to have a meaningful relationship with her parents. But they needed to put more effort into being better parents to her.

"Wow, I don't want you to feel like I hate you or anything. Regardless of the hurt feelings I have, you're still my father. And Sasha is my mother. I love both of you."

Chauncey hugged Sheila and held her tight as if she were a small child. She started to feel like she had been too hard on her parents and began to cry. Chauncey sensed this and pulled away from her embrace so that he could look into her eyes.

"Yo, what's wrong, why you crying?!"

"I just want us to put everything negative behind us and move forward!"

"Me too baby girl. I think I got an idea for a fresh start."

"What do you mean?"

"Yo, just come outside with me for a minute." Sheila followed him outside…

"You see that black car over there?" Sheila saw a black drop top Mercedes Benz parked in front of the house

"Wow, you doing it big like that!"

"No sweetheart, you doing it big."

He placed a set of car keys into her hand. "I know it doesn't make up for everything, but I love you and I want you to know that. Whatever I need to do to show you how much I love you, I will."

Sheila tried to hug him as tight as she could. "Oh my goodness, I can't believe this, thank you so much Chauncey! Can we take it for a test drive?!"

"Yo, did you hear what I said? This is your car, come on let's go."…

***

"Wow, I can't believe that your dad bought you a car!" Lashonda and Sheila were talking over the phone.

"Girl I know! And come on, a Mercedes Benz at that?!"

"So Sheila, where's your dad at now?"

"He's at my grandmother's house. He told me she's been sick and that I should make more attempts to go see her. So I'm going to start doing that."

"Yeah, that's still your grandmother. No matter how you think she feels about you. Life is way too short you know?"

"Hell yeah it is! You know my father asked me if I wanted to come to Philly during spring break. And I've really been thinking about going."

"I don't think it's a bad idea. Does your dad live with anyone, does he have a girlfriend?"

"He's with some chick named Candy. And she's only seven years older than me!"

"What, Sheila are you serious?!"

"Girl yes, I thought I told you about her? I'm sure I did, you just never remember shit!"

"Well tell me again!"

"Ok so to make a long story short, I met her about a year ago. My father called me one day to tell me he was in town. And he wanted to take me shopping. So he made plans to pick me up. You know me, I was all excited. When he arrived, I went to get in the car, and there was this skinny petite looking chick sitting in the front seat! She was a cute girl and all. But I was saying to myself, *who in the hell is this?* Then my father proceeded to tell me to get in the back seat. Immediately I felt like Candy should have been riding in the back. I mean I am his daughter! Anyways, he then says, *yo, this is Candy*. Now you know me Lashonda, I can be very sarcastic. So I said, *hello, and who are you to my father?*"

Lashonda laughed, "Sheila you a hot ass mess!"

"After that my father chimed in and told me that she was his girlfriend. And that they've been rocking together for about a year. Then he said he wanted us to meet and get to know each other. It was so awkward! I barely know him and now he's bringing this other woman around! It's like he wanted me to become best friends with her or something."

"Wow, that's a lot to handle Sheila!"

"Yeah it is! I'm just trying to stay positive because at the end of the day, I want to have a meaningful relationship with my father."

"Yes, I definitely understand. But you never told me if you liked Candy or not? Did you guys have a good vibe or was the whole thing just a disaster?"

"I can't really put my finger on it. I don't have anything against the girl. But I think the fact that she's young enough to be my big sister bothers me a little." The girls laugh aloud.

"You know what they say, you can't help who you love Sheila… So have your grandparents seen your new car yet?"

"No, they haven't gotten home from work yet. I wonder what they'll think. They might not even let me keep the car since I haven't completed a driver's education course."

"Girl relax, you're making a big deal out of nothing! And why wouldn't they let you keep the car, It's yours so why not?"

"Lashonda, you know my grandparents are aware of the type of lifestyle my father lives! Those reasons alone might cause my grandfather to flip out."

"Damn, well I hope not."

"Hold on Lashonda, somebody's calling on the other line." Sheila clicks over...

"Hello?"

"Hey beautiful, how are you?"

"Who is this?"

"It's me Lawrence, are you busy?"

Sheila's heart dropped, she was thrilled to get a call from him.

"No I'm not busy, hold on for a second ok?"

"Ok sweetheart," Sheila clicked back over to Lashonda.

"Girl, I got action on the other line!"

"What, who is it?"

"Do you remember I told you I met a guy at work last week named Lawrence?"

"Oh yeah, Mr. Dreamy with the caramel skin... Girl what did he say?"

"Well I won't know until I get off the phone with your ass!"

"Oh yeah right, well call me back and give me all the juicy details!"

"Ok I will, now bye!" ...

"Hello Lawrence?"

"Yes beautiful, I'm here."

Sheila loved his smooth sultry sounding voice. "I'm sorry to keep you waiting."

"Sweetheart for you, no amount of time is too long."

It seemed like whenever Sheila said anything, Lawrence would have the coolest comeback. She felt like clay in his hands, wanting him to mold and shape her however he wanted to. "So Lawrence, tell me about yourself, do you live around here?"

"Well, I'm from Cleveland and I graduated from The School of Arts. Right now I'm in my junior year of college in New York. But I come back and forth to visit my mom and family when I'm on break.

I'll be here for the next two months. And after that I go back to school in Rochester."

Sheila was intrigued by this guy. He was great looking, smart, and held a great conversation. "That's very impressive. It's a coincidence that you graduated from The School of Arts."

"Oh yeah, and why is that?"

"Well, I take Visual Art Communications at my high school."

"Oh ok, how old are you by the way?"

Sheila hesitated to answer the question. She wondered if he would feel uncomfortable since she was younger than him and still in high school. Surely he dated college girls who were much more mature than she was. "Oh, I'm almost eight-teen."

"Wow, I would have never guessed that, you seem so mature for your age."

"Thanks, I get that a lot." Sheila quickly embellished.

"So what are you looking to do with your art skills? Any particular area of Art you'd like to focus on?"

Sheila thought really hard for a moment. No one had ever asked her if she wanted to pursue Art as a career choice. "I haven't thought too much about it yet."

"Well you might want to start thinking about it. It's your senior year, and you have to know what you want to major in before you start college. If you want me to, I'd love to help you come up with a plan. And you can take advantage of freelance jobs as well. I have a graphic design business, and I work for myself."

Sheila felt like she was in a fairy tale and had met her prince charming. She wondered where this man had been all of her life. She had fallen for him after having only one phone conversation. He was introducing her to a world of business that she knew nothing about. "You have a lot of ambition Lawrence, and you're so motivating, I love it!"

"I appreciate that gorgeous, especially coming from you."

Sheila let out a flirtatious giggle. At this point Lawrence had her wrapped around his finger.

"When are you going to bless me with your presence again? I felt like we had such a magnetic energy when we met, and I would love to take you out this weekend."

Sheila immediately thought about Ryan. She felt guilty, almost like she was cheating on him. She really wanted to be loyal, but she knew on the other hand that she hated his lifestyle. Sheila wasn't sure if she could put her life on hold and wait for him.

Lawrence seemed like such a positive guy. And she needed the help he could give her in regards to a plan for college.

"Yeah, I'm available this weekend."

"Well this weekend it is. I'll set up something nice so that we can just enjoy each other's company and have a good time."

"That sounds great Lawrence."

"Ok, well text me your address, and I'll see you this weekend."

"Alright, I will."…

***

Frank arrived home later that evening. As he approached his yard, he noticed a black Mercedes parked in the front of his house. He quickly went into the house where he was greeted by Sheila sitting on the sofa.

"Hey Daddy," Sheila said as she got up to give him a hug. "I have something I want to talk to you about."

"Oh no, what now Sheila?"

Nora arrived as well. She gave Frank a quick kiss and sat on the sofa with him and Sheila.

"Ma, you came in at just the right time! I have to talk to both of you about something."

"Ok, go for it."

"Well for starters, Chauncey stopped by to see me earlier today."

"Chauncey came to see you?"

"Yes Ma, and I wasn't expecting to see him either."

"Well, what did he want?"

"Ma he told me that he was here visiting his mother because she's sick. He also mentioned that he wanted me to make more attempts to visit her."

Frank laughed out loud. "Last time I checked you were the child and she was the adult. She should be reaching out to you!"

"Frank, two wrongs don't make a right. I think it's good that her father wanted to see her. And it's good that he wants her to spend more time with Jill."

"Exactly Ma! So anyway, we were talking about a lot of other things as well. He also mentioned that he wanted me to come to

Philly with him this spring so that I can meet some of my other family members, and -"

"Wait a minute, did you say go to Philly?"

"Yes Daddy, Philly."

"Now Sheila, you know that's a huge step! You've only been around your father a handful of times."

Ok Ma, you guys are over reacting right now. You haven't even given him a chance!"

"You listen to me Sheila. I'm not trying to come in between a relationship with you and your father. But at the same time there has to be some level of trust built here! He can't just come in and completely take over. We barely even know him! He could be a damn pervert for all we know!"

"Daddy seriously though, now you're just hitting below the belt!"

"Sheila, Frank is right! First of all, Chauncey shouldn't have even had this conversation with you! We're the ones that have been raising you for the last seventeen years, not him! You would think he'd at least have the decency and common sense to consult with us before making all of these plans without our knowledge or consent!"

"I just feel like I'm already the odd ball at school because all of my friends grew up with their parents and I didn't."

"Sheila, you are blessed and you don't even realize it! Do you know how many kids would love to be in your position? We took you in, but you could have been given up for adoption! We weren't going to let that happen to you, but I don't think you appreciate any of that!"

"But Ma I do!"

"Well Chauncey is going to have to sit down with us, have a discussion, and gain our trust!"

"'I agree with that too Daddy! But now I don't know how to bring up what I want to say next!"

"Well you might as well just lay it all on us Sheila."

"Ok Ma, so did y'all see that black Benz outside when you came home?"

Frank frowned as he recollected seeing the car parked out front. "Yeah I did, what about it?"

"Well, Chauncey bought that car for me!"

Frank and Nora quickly got up from their seats and rushed to the window to look at the car. "What do you mean he bought it for you? That's an expensive car for a young girl like you. This is exactly what we were talking about! He gives a car to a teenager, instead of telling us he wanted to give you a car?!"

"Yeah Sheila, I really don't like how he goes around us to go straight to you. What me and your grandfather think doesn't even matter to him it seems like!"

Sheila slumped down onto the couch. She knew it would be hard for her grandparents to accept the fact that her father got her a new car... "So let me guess, y'all not going to let me keep the car, are you?"

"I'll tell you one thing for sure. You won't be driving any car until you've completed a driver's education course. You also have to make sure you keep up with your school work. And come up with a solid plan for what you want to do after high school."

Sheila was thrilled. All of the conditions her grandparents gave her in order to keep the car were fair and within reason.

"Absolutely, I will definitely do all of those things, no problem!"

"That's not all to it!" Nora added.

"What do you mean?"

"What I mean is that we still need to talk to your father. And until he can build a solid trustworthy relationship with us, you have to give him the car back."

"I agree with Nora, It's the right thing to do. Your father needs to understand that there's an order and a way to do things properly. And trying to shower you with expensive gifts isn't going to make up for all the years that he wasn't around."

Sheila threw her hands up in despair. "Daddy are ya'll serious?!"

"We're very serious! Your grandfather and I just don't think you should accept something like that. We need to have an understanding of Chauncey and who he is. And he needs to talk to your mother and get the ok from her about you going to Philadelphia."

Sheila got up from her seat and began to cry. "Why are you going to leave that up to her? She hasn't been in my life either and he's done more for me financially than she ever has!"

"Money don't mean shit! Your mother cares about your life and your safety at the end of the day, that's why she left you with us!"

Sheila looked at her grandfather and was completely astounded. She never imagined that he would agree with Nora about anything concerning Sasha. What Sheila didn't know was that Frank remembered the letter Sasha wrote when she ran away years ago. And he remembered her saying that she didn't want Sheila around Chauncey. So for that reason he was just trying to play things safe…"You know what fine, it doesn't matter. I know that Chauncey won't have a problem doing any of this! And both of you will see that all of this was unnecessary."…

***

It was the weekend. Nora and Frank were both working. Sheila was getting ready for her date with Lawrence. She didn't know where they were going exactly. But she figured since he was in college, he might want to take her somewhere sophisticated. She wore jeans and a fitted blouse with her hair pulled up into a bun. It gave her a casual look, ready for any occasion. Suddenly there was a knock at the door and her heart fluttered. At that moment, she realized that she had never been taken out on a real date before. Mainly because her grandparents never told her that she could date.

Sheila hurried downstairs to meet Lawrence at the door. He had a beautiful bouquet of red roses and he was dressed to impress. He had this classy urban look going on with his attire.

"Wow, you look gorgeous Sheila!" He wasted no time pulling her slim waist towards him and kissing her on the cheek. "These roses are for you."

"These are beautiful Lawrence, thank you!"
"Of course, are you ready to go?"
"Yeah I am."
He took her by the hand and led her to his car…

Twenty minutes later they arrived at an art gallery. Sheila was glad that she dressed appropriately since she didn't know what the evening called for. Lawrence acted as a gentleman the entire night. He opened doors for her everywhere they went. And he always took her by the hand to lead the way. He was just an absolute prince charming and Sheila couldn't get enough of him.

As they walked through the elaborate Art Gallery, Lawrence held Sheila's hand the entire time. He also explained all of the art pieces to her as they examined them.

"So what do you think of this place?"

It was Sheila's first time going to an art gallery, so she had a million thoughts running through her mind. "I think it's great! I have no idea what type of career in art I'd like to have though. I just know that I like to draw. I'm good at it, but I never really thought about how I could monetize off of it."

"Well first of all, you have to change your mind set."

"What do you mean Lawrence?"

"You just said that you don't know how to monetize off of your artwork right?"

"Well, yeah."

"Art is an expression of who you are, what you love, and what you stand for. True artist aren't in it for the money. We do it for the passion and the freedom of expression that it gives us. Take me for example. I'm a black man from the inner city, and my attire clearly shows that. Most people would think that I'm a thug because of how I dress. It's like people have these preconceived notions without even knowing you. My attire is a part of my art, and it enables me to control how people see me. It gives me the freedom to express myself and show how I want to be perceived. Unless you knew me, you wouldn't know that I like Jazz and Classical music. I also like Hip Hop and R&B too. See, that's the beauty of being an artist! You get to paint all these different pictures of yourself on a canvas! I control the brush on my canvas. I also control my destination in life. Sheila, I want you to be able to tap into that same power."

Sheila was completely amazed. Lawrence spoke such great swelling words, and her heart was set on being with him. She tried to keep her cool, not wanting him to know how weak she was for him. "Yes Lawrence, I do want to tap into that power." He gazed into her hazel brown eyes. And before she knew it, his hand was behind her neck and his lips were kissing hers. Gripping her passionately with every embrace...

That feels so good

Winter break arrived, and Sheila was out of school for the next two weeks. It had been an interesting year so far. Chauncey finally met with Nora and Frank to discuss Sheila's future. He assured them that her college tuition would be taken care of, and that they'd have nothing to worry about. He came to visit from Philly every other weekend, but Nora and Frank were still trying to figure out if his intentions were genuine. Once they began to see how committed he was to visiting often, their views changed. They saw him put forth real effort and decided that it was ok for her to go visit him in Philly. They also let Sheila keep the car that he bought for her.

***

"Now you make sure that you call us as soon as your flight lands."

"Yes Mam, I hear you loud and clear for the fiftieth time."

"Hey now, don't you get all sassy. We're just trying to make sure that you're going to be safe. It's a lot of crazy people out here in the world. So don't get on that plane talking to any strangers. Just sit your ass down, be quiet, and get to where you need to go."

"Oh my goodness Daddy, y'all act like I'm not seventeen years old. Seriously though, this is embarrassing!"

Flight 547, your flight is now boarding, flight 547 your flight is now boarding. A flight attendant broadcasted over the airport intercom.

"Oh that's me, that's my flight I have to go!"

"I'm going to miss you so much! I hope you're going to be ok." Nora placed her hand on Sheila's cheek, as if she was going to cry.

Frank wrapped his arm around Nora.

"The girl is only going to be gone for ten days. She'll be back before you know it."

"Daddy's right Ma, everything will be fine, trust me!" Sheila reached over to hug her grandmother and kissed her on the cheek.

"Ok, now get going before you miss your flight. Nora and I will be waiting for you to call us when you land."

Sheila kissed her grandfather on the cheek. "Love y'all, talk to you soon!"

"We love you too baby, and call us as soon as you land!"

"I will Ma!"

Nora and Frank watched Sheila walk down the jet way until she was out of sight…"I hope we're not making a big mistake by letting her go visit him."

"I hope not either Nora, for Chauncey's sake…"

Sheila boarded the plane and got a seat next to the window. It was her first time flying on an airplane. She couldn't believe she was going to visit her father in Philadelphia. Her sixteen year old brother Cartier lived there too. Sheila figured it would be good to spend some time with him as well. As she seated herself on the plane, the flight attendant approached her.

"Hello Ms. and thank you for flying first class with Continental! Today we have Chicken Cordon Bleu for lunch, or a Chicken Caesar salad, which Entree can I get for you?"

Sheila had no idea what first class was, and she definitely had never heard of Chicken Cordon Bleu. Instantly she felt out of place. The flight attendant interrupted her thoughts. "Hello, Ms.?"

"Um yes, I'm sorry. I'm not sure which one to choose?"

"May I recommend the Chicken Caesar Salad? It's made with crisp romaine lettuce, ripe tomatoes, grated parmesan cheese, and it's dressed with our own blended Caesar. How does that sound?"

"Yeah sure, that sounds fine."

"Great, I'll have that ready for you momentarily." The attendant moved on to take the next passenger's order.

Sheila grabbed her headphones and began listening to music. As she was slowly drifting off to sleep, she thought about Lawrence. They'd been dating for about three months now. He would come back and forth from Rochester periodically to visit, and things were going great between them. She introduced him to her grandparents and they loved him. Nora and Frank were impressed by him being in college and having his own graphic design business. It overshadowed the fact that he was five years older than Sheila. Nora was glad that he helped her with college applications and choosing a curriculum for the fall. Sheila was head over heels for him, but she couldn't enjoy it. She felt guilty because technically she was still with Ryan. And she promised that she would wait on him to come home from jail. He ended up getting sentenced to three years in prison for gun charges and possession of drugs. It was as if everything was getting worse for him. And his outlook on life was terrible. All he talked about was how he couldn't wait to come home so he could reclaim the streets and make a name for himself. Sheila was tired of his whole lifestyle and she knew she could never really live a life like that. But she could easily see herself being with Lawrence and building a life with him. All these thoughts ran through her mind as she laid her head back, listening to the singer Monica playing in her headphones.

***

Sheila's plane landed a few hours later. Once she exited the plane, she waited at curbside for Chauncey to pick her up. While waiting, she decided to call her grandparents to let them know she landed safely… "Hey Ma, it's me Sheila!"

"Hey honey! I'm so glad you landed safely!"

"Yeah Ma, the flight was quick and everything went good."…

"Yo Sheila!"

Sheila turned around to see her father yelling out her name, trying to get her attention. "Hey Ma, Chauncey is here to pick me up, so I'll call you later ok?"

"Ok, love you Sheila! You be safe and I'll talk to you later!"…

Chauncey was driving a 2003 tan colored Cadillac sitting on 20 inch rims with tinted windows. And it had a sun roof. It was a flashy car with tan leather interior and it was fully loaded. Every time she saw her father he was always in a different ride. She then saw her brother sitting in the backseat. He got out of the car and greeted her with a hug.

"What's up big head!" Cartier stood 6ft with hazel brown eyes and brush waves. Chauncey was dark skinned, while Cartier was more fair skinned like his mom. He was built like a basketball player while Chauncey was stocky and muscular, more so built like a football player. Nonetheless, anyone could clearly see that Cartier looked just like his father.

"What, big head? Boy please, that head of yours is wider than the equator!" Sheila and Cartier laugh.

"Come on, let's roll out." Chauncey replied as they all got into the car…

"Yo, look at Sheila. My baby girl is all grown up!"

"I'm definitely all grown up!"

"Yo, not just yet, pump them brakes! You still got some growing up to do. How was your flight by the way?"

Sheila looked over at her father. He was so laid back and cool. He would drive with one hand on the steering wheel stretched forward, while reclined back in his seat. He definitely was the king of swag, and it was hard for Sheila to look at him as the disciplinary type of parent. He was more like a friend or a big brother.

"Oh, the flight was cool. Chauncey, I just want to say thank you so much for everything! The new car and this trip. I'm just happy to be here with you and Cartier. This means so much to me."

"Ah, listen to daddy's lil pooh pooh."

Sheila couldn't stop laughing at her father joking.

"Well, since you're only here for ten days, I figured we'd take a road trip down to Florida. So you can meet some of your other family members."

"That would be great Chauncey!"

"Yeah, I thought so too. Plus I ain't been down there in a while myself. I got a few moves I could make while we're there…So what ya'll want to eat?"

"Dad, do you really have to ask?"

"What you mean Cartier?"

"How are you not going to take Sheila to Jakes and get her a real Philly cheese steak sandwich?"

"Hold up now, I've had a real Philly cheese steak before! They sell those back home at Mr. Heroes!" Cartier and Chauncey burst out into laughter. "What's so funny?"

"Yo, Mr. Heroes don't know shit about making a real Philly cheese steak! They don't even use real steak meat! All that shit is processed and it's fake meat. I see your pops got a lot to teach you."

"Oh whatever," Said Sheila as Chauncey drove them all to Jakes. A famous steak house on the east side of Philly...

After dinner, Chauncey arrived to his house. He lived about forty five minutes outside of the city. It was a suburban neighborhood. He had a modest ranch style home, which was a little opposite of what he portrayed with his elaborate cars, clothes, and jewelry.

"Yo Cartier, grab your sister's bags and take them inside the house while we talk for a minute."

"Ok pops,"...

"Sheila look, I just want you to know that all of this is long overdue. You should have BEEN here with me and a part of my life. I feel bad about that, and I want you to feel like this is your home too."

"Chauncey I do, and there are no hard feelings. All that matters is that I'm here now and we're starting a new beginning."

"You know Sheila, you're very mature for your age. Your mother use to be that way when we were younger. How she been doing anyway?"

Sheila sighed upon him mentioning Sasha. "She's fine I guess."

"What you mean you guess, don't you talk to her?" Chauncey and Sasha hadn't spoken in years ever since he found out she dated Mark. And to make matters worse, Mark ended up dumping Sasha two years after she left with him to go to Florida. He also told Chauncey that Sasha came on to him, and that it was only about sex between the two of them.

"Well, she called a few months ago and said that she's moving back to Cleveland. How exciting that's going to be." Sheila said sarcastically, Chauncey laughed at her response.

"Yo, at the end of the day that's still your mother. I know we haven't been the best parents to you, but we have always loved you and wanted the best for you. I'm a street nigga, and your mother was in the streets. But you know, I'm in a better position to play a better role in your life now. Besides, Frank was good for you. And that's what you needed as a father figure. He gave you what I couldn't."

Sheila was taken back by everything her father was saying to her. She respected it, but at the same time she instantly resented him. She wondered how her parents could be so caught up in the streets and not be parents to her. And seeing her brother Cartier live with Chauncey didn't make it any easier to accept. He had always lived with him, and Sheila felt like there was some favoritism involved. But in spite of all these thoughts that were racing through her head, she figured now wasn't the time to mention any of it. She just nodded her head in agreement with him. "Yeah, you're right Chauncey."

"Yo, with all that being said, you need to know that Candy lives here too."

"Oh really, she lives here?"

"Well you should know by now that she's my main girl. And she's been rocking with your pops for a while now. She's solid, stable, you know, she a good team player." Sheila's mind was going crazy at this point, and she felt like her father put everyone before her. "I figured since I'll be working these last few days before we take this road trip, Candy could show you around the city and take you shopping. I want you two to get to know each other. I need the two most important women in my life to be close." Chauncey opened his car door, and then came around to open Sheila's door for her.

Sheila felt almost heartbroken. She remembered her father telling her that she was the most important woman in his life. But now she had to share that spot with Candy...

"Oh my goodness, Sheila look at you!"

It was Candy, greeting Sheila with open arms as soon as she walked into the house. Sheila was not prepared to have to deal with Candy, she thought her father lived alone. It made her feel uncomfortable because she had to pretend that she liked Candy. She definitely wasn't a fan of her to say the least.

Chauncey sensed Sheila's tension towards Candy and quickly jumped in the conversation. "Yo, Sheila got prom coming up, maybe you can take her to some of the boutiques out here and help her find a dress."

"Oh I'd love to! That would be so much fun, wouldn't it Sheila?!"

"Oh yea, tons of fun."...

"Sheila, you've grown up to be a beautiful young lady, and your hair is gorgeous!" Sheila was a splitting image of Sasha in her younger days. She was tall with a slim shaped body, and had long shoulder length black hair. A lot of people often told her that she looked like the super model Tyra Banks. And she had beautiful hazel brown eyes.

"Yo, I need to take off for a little while, but I'll be back later Sheila."

"Um, ok?" Sheila couldn't believe her father was already leaving after she had just gotten there.

"Don't worry Sheila, you're in good hands! You've got me to show you around the city. We're going to have so much fun!" Sheila tried to force a smile on her face.

"Come on, I'll show you your room big head." Cartier said as he led Sheila to her room...

***

It was the next morning and Sheila was awakened to the smell of fresh brewing coffee. She went downstairs and saw Candy getting ready to leave for work.

"Good morning sweetie!"

"Good morning Candy."

"How did you sleep?"

"I slept ok. Is my father awake yet?"

"Honey, your father is an early bird. He's been gone ever since 5 a.m."

"He's been gone since 5 a.m., why so early?!"

"All I can say is that your father lives in a world of his own. I'm just glad he found a place for me to fit in!" Candy grabbed her cup of coffee and sat down on the couch next to Sheila. Then she placed her hand on Sheila's lap. "I just need you to know that I really respect you and your mother. And I'm not trying to be your mom, I just want to be your friend."

"Yeah, I know that Candy. I never thought you were trying to be my mother. And I appreciate you saying that." Sheila felt like maybe she had been too hard on Candy and that she should give her a chance. Besides, she seemed like a nice person and hadn't given Sheila any reason not to like her.

"Well good! I'm glad I got that off my chest. I feel like we can have a fresh start now. I'm off from work at 3:30. Do you want to go shopping later?"

"Hell yeah I do!"

"Ok so shopping it is, see you when I get off!" Candy kissed Sheila on the cheek and headed out the door for work...

"What's up big head?" Cartier joked with Sheila as he came downstairs.

"Cartier, I thought you were on winter break?!"

"Nah man, we still got two more days left!"

"Ah, that's terrible!"

"Yeah it is!" He grabbed a pop tart from the toaster and headed for the door. "See you later sis!"

"Bye Cartier," *Well this is going to be a boring ass morning.* Sheila thought to herself as she went upstairs to go back to sleep...

It was around 4 p.m. when Sheila's cell phone rang. She looked to see who it was, but didn't recognize the number. "Hello?"

"Hey Sheila, it's me Candy."

"Hey Candy, what's up?"

"I got your number from your dad. Are you dressed and ready to go?"

"Yeah I am."

"Ok well I'm outside. Come on out so we can go."

"Ok here I come." Sheila grabbed her purse and rushed down the stairs, then out the door...

"Wow, there are hardly any fast food places in Philly!" Sheila complained as she stared out her passenger window while Candy drove.

"Yeah, Philly is a lot different from Cleveland. Most of the people here like to eat authentic food. You won't find too many fast food places around here."

Sheila noticed that there were a lot of run down abandoned buildings in the city. And there were a lot of one way streets as well.

It seemed a lot grimier than her neighborhood back home. Finally they arrived at a shopping mall.

"So, do you have a date for the prom yet Sheila?"

"Well, I was supposed to go with my boyfriend, but he's, well, he's in jail."

Candy took a swift look at Sheila. "He's in jail?!"

"Yeah I know. And please don't tell my father, he would kill me!"

Candy began to laugh. "Sweetheart, your father probably isn't too much different from your boyfriend in jail."

Sheila looked confused. "What do you mean by that?"

"Don't get me wrong, your father is a good man. But he has this life out in the streets, and only God knows what it truly consists of."

Candy's statement made Sheila wonder. It seemed like Candy really didn't like the lifestyle her father was into but yet she still dated him. "So how did you end up with my father, if you don't agree with his lifestyle?"

Candy squinted her eyes at Sheila's question. "Well sweetie, that's not the case at all. You're father approached me, and when we met he was running the auto body shop. So I thought that's all he did. Let's just say I had to find things out the hard way about your dad."

"Oh, well it just seems like the two of you are so different. How did y'all end up together?"

"I'll let you in on a little secret. When I met your dad, I was still with the father of my children".

"You have kids, where are they?! I didn't know you had any!"

"They stay with their dad during the week since he lives closer to their school. I get them on the weekends. You'll get to meet them when they come with us to Florida later this week."

"So what happened with you and their father? I mean if you don't mind me asking."

"No, of course I don't mind! Their father and I were like high school sweethearts. We went to prom together, and we had this whole life planned out. When he went to college, the plan was for me to watch the kids while he got his degree. And then he would let me go to college and finish school when he was done. Well, it definitely didn't work out that way! When he got out of college he didn't want me to go back to school or work. He just wanted me to stay home and take care of the kids."

"And you had a problem with that?"

"I know it sounds crazy Sheila, but that's not what I wanted at all! Whatever I wanted, he gave it to me. Whatever I told him to do, he would do it. And it just made me feel like he was so weak. I felt like I could just walk all over him! That's not the type of man that I want."

"Wow, it seems like the type of man that every girl wants!"

"Yeah, that's what I thought too. But then I realized I needed a strong man that could tell me no, and not let me control him. Sheila, your father is a good man. And his authority is what attracted me to him."

"Well I'm glad it all worked out for you."

"It did, and he's great with my boys! They look at him like a father!" Sheila looked down, feeling pained. She wondered why her father never interacted with her like that.

"Hey you," Candy took her hand and placed it under Sheila's chin to raise her head. "You know your father loves you too right?" "Yeah I know." Sheila quickly changed the subject. "Oh look, Victoria's Secret, can we go in there?"

"Of course we can. Come on, let's go"...

Sheila saw a pink bra and panty lace set in the store. It was really pretty and she wanted it. "Can you please buy me this?"

Candy observed the set. "Do you know your exact bra and panty size?"

Sheila looked confused. "I mean, I put it up to my chest. It looked like it fits."

Candy laughed at her comment. "Honey you have to try this on!"

Sheila looked in amazement as if Candy had just said something bizarre to her. "Try it on, you can't try on underwear, that's disgusting!" Sheila had never been to Victoria's Secret. She just always went to Walmart with Nora to buy her underwear.

Candy took her by the hand and led her to the back of the store where she could get her bra and panty size taken. Then she tried on the bra and panty set...

"How does it fit?" Candy asked from outside of the dressing room.

"I don't know, it's a little tight. And it makes everything so propped up on me!"

"Honey it's supposed to prop everything up. Come on out, let me see how you look."

Sheila was very shy. Her grandmother had never even seen her in bra and panties by accident. And here Candy was, asking to see her willingly. "Ok," said Sheila while still skeptical.

"Honey it's only women in here, you have nothing to be shy about."

Sheila walked out of the dressing room with her arms crossed, covering her chest. Candy's jaw practically dropped when she saw her. "Oh my goodness, you look so good in your bra and panties!" She came towards Sheila and grabbed her breasts. "This bra makes your breast look so perky!" She then walked behind her and grabbed the sides of her waist. "You are beautiful, just like your mom. And you have lovely curves."

"Ok, I'm going to change now Candy."

"Give me your bra and panty set so I can pay for it."

***

"Yo, what's up?" It was Chauncey calling Candy from the shop.

"Hey love, are you on your way home yet?"

"Is that my father?" Sheila interrupted as she overheard Candy on the phone.

"Yeah, this is him."

"I'm probably going to be late coming home, I got a few moves to make with Mark real quick."

"Come on Chauncey, you said you were going to come home early this week, especially since Sheila is here."

"Yo, you need to chill with all that while my daughter around. She don't need to hear that."

"Chauncey, I'm just –"

"Nah, you just said enough already Candy. I'll see you when I get home." Chauncey hung up the phone.

Candy stayed on the phone for a moment after he hung up. She was embarrassed and felt like Chauncey had no respect for her.

"Well, what did he say?"

"He's not on his way yet. But he should be here shortly though." Candy lied to try and smooth things over, knowing how much Sheila wanted to spend time with her father…

***

It was 11 p.m. later that night. Sheila and Candy had eaten their dinner, and were about to go to bed. Cartier left a note on the refrigerator saying that he was spending the night at a friend's house. Sheila was lying in her room watching television when Candy was getting out of the shower. Then Candy called for Sheila from the other room. "Sheila, can you come here for a minute?"

"Yeah here I come." She got up from her bed and went across the hall to Chauncey and Candy's room. Candy was sitting on her bed naked with her body still slightly wet from her shower. "Girl, why you call me in here while you aint got no clothes on?!" Sheila stood there stuck, not knowing rather to walk away or stay and wait for a response.

Candy got up from the bed, fully exposing her slender fair skinned body. She had petite perky breast and an ass shaped like a heart. She stood about 5'6". Her lips were full and her hair was cut into a short bob. She was a beautiful woman, and Sheila began to feel weird. "Sheila, why are you so nervous about you're sexuality? You're a beautiful woman, and other women are beautiful too. You shouldn't be ashamed of that."

"Ok Candy, anyway what do you want?" Sheila was clearly agitated. She didn't like the ill feelings she was having. And at this point she just wanted to go back to her room.

"Honey, I've had such a long day, I just need a massage. Normally your dad or brother would be here to give me one."

Sheila was surprised at what Candy just said. "Wait, my brother massages you while you're naked?!"

Candy giggled as she lied across the bed flat on her stomach. Sheila then noticed the stretch marks that were on her butt cheeks. There were rows and rows of them, lighter than her overall skin complexion. They almost seemed strategically placed, as if they were painted on, like a purposeful design. "Come here and just massage my back for five minutes please." Sheila felt like she was in some sort of trance under Candy's every command. It made her feel confused. She went over to the bed and reached down while still standing up to massage Candy's back. "Sit across me so that you can get better leverage silly." Sheila was hesitant, but she straddled herself across Candy's ass and began massaging her back. She started with her shoulders, and then worked her way down the sides of her back. She penetrated Candy's skin graciously with her fingertips. "Oh, that feels so good." Candy said in a moaning sensual tone…

Dirty Little Secrets

It was the third day into Sheila's trip to Philly. Chauncey and Cartier were outside loading up the black Suburban with everyone's luggage. Candy and Sheila were in the house packing food for the trip.

"Yo hurry up, we on a time schedule!" Chauncey yelled from outside.

"Ok, here we come! Come on babe, your dad is ready and when he's in a rush, he's not a happy man."

Sheila and Candy had this new found friendship. Candy gave her relationship advice on guys, and showed her how to dress sexy, but still classy. Sheila loved feeling like she had someone older to show her the ropes and the ways of being a woman.

"So Sheila, are you nervous about the trip and meeting your family?"

"Nervous is an understatement!"

"Sweetie, you'll be fine! You're a beautiful girl and they're going to love you!"

"Yeah, I hope so. Cartier has it made so easy! Everyone already knows him in the family! And I'm like the black sheep that no one ever speaks of."

Candy put her arm around Sheila's shoulder. "Babe, your father and I have had many conversations about this, and he knows that he made a lot of mistakes. I know that he loves you and Cartier equally. It's just a complicated situation, since he actually had a relationship with Tameka, you know?"

"What do you mean? He had a relationship with my mother too!"

"Well babe, it really doesn't matter at this point, it was such a long time ago. I was just always under the impression that Chauncey was in a meaningful relationship with Cartier's mom. I think he just sort of hooked up with your mom for the moment. Honey we all have those moments, so it's nothing to be embarrassed about. It's a part of life, look what came out of it. You were the beautiful blessing!" Candy grabbed the food they packed and left Sheila standing in the kitchen feeling angry, embarrassed, and humiliated.

***

It had been a nineteen hour road trip from Philadelphia to Orlando, and everyone was exhausted. They would have gotten there a lot sooner if it weren't for Chauncey taking the wrong route three times. They were on their way to meet up with his sister. Sheila didn't know how to feel. She was excited about the trip at first, but she still couldn't get over the comment Candy made about Chauncey's relationship with Sasha. It made her feel as if she was some type of unwanted mistake. Sheila just felt a deep sense of gloom and listened to her headphones on the entire car ride. Chauncey finally arrived at his sister's gated community. Judging from the Italian décor and water fountains, you could easily assume that the people who stayed here were wealthy…

"Candy I haven't seen Trina in a few years. She's going to be mad I took this long to come down here."

"Well hopefully since Sheila is here that will take some of the heat off of you."

"Hey little brother!" Trina greeted Chauncey with open arms when she saw him. There were six of them altogether, but they were the closest among all of their siblings.

"Yo Trina how you been?!"

"I've been just fine. And look at this beautiful family you have!" She looked around at everyone and then focused her attention on Sheila. "Is this little brown eyed Sheila?" Trina got teary eyed as she reached around everyone else to get to Sheila. "It's been years since I've seen you, you're beautiful, absolutely stunning!"

Sheila instantly got a sense of relief and felt a little reassurance from her aunt's response towards her. She thought to herself that the trip might not end up being so bad after all. Trina took them all inside where they spent the next five hours talking with family. Sheila was introduced to all of her cousins, and ate a huge dinner that her aunt prepared for them...

It was close to midnight when Chauncey left his sister's house. He arrived at the hotel and waited for valet.

"Why are you valet parking, shouldn't you just use the garage? We're not going back out tonight."

"Yo, me and Cartier about to go handle some business real quick and peep the scenes. So we can see what's popping out here."

"What?! Well let me and Sheila come with you!"

"Candy, don't start this shit. I'm not about to take my daughter out to no fucking club!"

"Oh, so that's where you're going? That's the business you need to handle, and you're taking your sixteen year old son with you? Sheila is a year older than him and more mature! So why can't she go too?!"

"Yo Candy, don't do this right now, it's not even up for discussion." He motioned for a parking attendant to carry their bags into the hotel. Then he tipped the man fifty dollars. "Take Sheila upstairs, me and Cartier will be back later."

Candy tried to give him the most distasteful look that she could. Then she got out of the truck and slammed the door. Sheila didn't even try to contest with her father. She was intimidated by his dominating demeanor.

***

Candy had been crying ever since she got to the hotel room. Four hours had passed since Chauncey dropped them off and he still hadn't come back. Candy was calling him constantly, but he wasn't answering her calls. Sheila tried to sleep but was unable to because she could hear Candy's weeping through her bedroom walls. She decided to get up to try and console her as best as she could. She went into Candy's room and sat down next to her on the bed.

"What's wrong?" Obviously Sheila already knew why Candy was upset.

"I just don't know what I should be expecting from your father! One minute he's doing everything right and then the next minute he goes right back to his old ways! I really don't understand it! I love him so much, but he's forcing me to make a decision that I don't want to make! I don't know what to do! I can't live without him. I just want him to do right by me the way that I do right by him!"

Sheila took Candy by the hand. "Candy, look at me. You have to know your self-worth and know what you deserve. Chauncey is my father, but if he's not treating you right, then you need to reevaluate the relationship!"

"You're right Sheila."

"Come on, let's go into the living room and watch TV."

Once in the living room, Sheila plopped down onto the couch. Candy took a seat at the dining room table. Then she pulled out a box of black and mild cigars from her purse.

"Candy you smoke?"

"Sweetie, your father has me going back to a lot of shit that I use to do. I just can't believe we're going through this, we just got over a huge ordeal!"

"What do you mean?"

"Your father is the master of manipulation! One day last month, I was cleaning out the garage, and I heard this beeping sound. So I tried to figure out where the hell it was coming from. I look behind his tool box, and I see a pager, wrapped up in rags!"

"What in the hell was it doing there?!"

"I know Sheila, that's the same thing I said! So I went in the house, dialed the number, and some young sounding female answered the phone! Then I asked her, *did someone page Chauncey?* And do you know she had the nerve to ask me who was I? Then she asked me why I had her man's pager! I mean seriously, the audacity of this bitch, calling my man her man!"

"Wow, what happened next?!"

"Well I asked her, *sweetheart, how is he your man when he lives with me and comes home to me every night?! We have a life and a family together! So please explain to me how he's your man?* Then she goes on to ask me if I knew Deonte and Darryl!"

"Oh shit, she knew your kid's names?!"

"Exactly, the bitch told me her and Chauncey had been dating for eight months! She also said that he told her Deonte and Darryl were his little brothers. And that he just helps his mom out by taking them to school every morning!"

Sheila couldn't believe what she was hearing about her father. Although she wasn't surprised, she still didn't want to believe it.

Candy began to sob all over again while Sheila tried to console her. "He has no respect for me or my kids! Why would he even have them around another woman?"

"So who is this chick Candy, where is she from?!"

Candy laughed sarcastically. "It's funny that you ask Sheila. I noticed that the girl had an accent. So I asked her where she's from, and she told me that she's from Korea! But Sheila, the worst part is that she's only seven-teen years old!"

"Wait, What?!" Sheila was disgusted at the thought of her father dating a girl her age.

"By now Sheila, me and this girl weren't even mad at each other anymore. I mean how could we be?! Chauncey was clearly playing the both of us! The girl started practically crying like a baby over the phone! And she said that he hadn't called her in weeks ever since she got his name tattooed on her thigh!" Candy then showed Sheila a tattoo of Chauncey's name on her upper chest.

"Oh my goodness, you got my dad's name tatted on you too?" Sheila was at a complete loss for words. Candy didn't even seem like the type of woman that would tolerate a man like her father. She seemed like a classy chick, while Chauncey was rough and rigid. They were truly two peas from a different pod...

It was morning time. Candy had fallen asleep on the couch after crying all night. And Sheila finally managed to doze off somewhere around 5 a.m. The guys must have snuck in during the wee hours of the morning while the girls were sleeping. Chauncey made plans with Trina to meet up at Universal studios later that day so everyone could hang out. But judging by the silent treatment Candy was giving him, it didn't look like the day was off to a good start...

"Candy, you aint said shit to me all day, what's up?" Everyone was riding in the Suburban truck on their way to Universal Studios.

"Do you really have to ask Chauncey? You don't think I have a reason to be mad?"

"What I think is that you're over reacting! This trip is supposed to be about me and my daughter reconnecting, and you just killing everybody's vibe yo! I'm out here spending all this money so we can have a good time. But all you wanna do is nag a nigga about nothing! I'm not trying to hear that shit Candy! You act like I can't even take a piss without you knowing about it!" Candy motioned for him to lower his tone. Chauncey looked into his rear view mirror to see if Sheila or Cartier heard what he said. But they had been riding with their headphones on the entire time. "Look, when we pull up, try to relax. Don't let Trina think we got problems going on."

"Whatever you say Chauncey." …

"Hey there baby brother!" Trina hugged Chauncey at the entrance of Universal Studios. She brought her kids with her as well. Then she turned her attention to Candy. "So Candy, what are we going to do first, the waterslides? You know it's great out here this time of year."

Candy dreaded the thought of having to fake being happy for the entire day. So she came up with a scheme to get herself out of the date. Out of nowhere, she let out a slight moan and began bending over and hugging her stomach.

"Honey, are you ok?"

Candy looked up at Trina with a grief stricken face. "Oh Trina, I think I'll be ok. I just got my period and these cramps are killing me, I can barely walk!"

"Sweetie why are you even here! Oh you poor thing, you should be back at the hotel and in bed!" Trina slapped Chauncey on his arm. "Boy, why did you let her come out feeling like this? Can't you see the girl is clearly in pain?!"

Candy struggled to hold back her laughs. Her lie was working just as she had planned. And it didn't hurt to see Chauncey get some much needed scolding.

"Yo sis, she wanted to come!"

"He's right Trina, we don't get to see you guys that often. And it would be selfish of me to cancel everyone's plans, just because of me and some cramps."

"Oh don't you be silly Candy!" She wrapped her arm around Candy's shoulder. "I'm going to drive you back to the hotel, and you are going to relax for the day!"

"Sis Candy is a grown woman, she can take care of herself." Chauncey knew what Candy was up to and he didn't like the way she was manipulating his sister.

"Oh no, I live here, so I know the quickest route to get to the hotel and back! You just take Cartier and Sheila with you. Candy's boys and my boys can go with you as well. It should only take me about twenty minutes to get to the hotel and back."

"Well, if you insist." Chauncey said in a dry tone.

"Come on Candy, let's get you back to the hotel so you can relax and get some rest!"

Chauncey and everyone else headed towards the Universal Studios entrance to go in…

"How you enjoying the trip so far Sheila?"

"Oh its ok, I guess."

"Wow, it's just ok huh? Yo, I've been going out of my way to show you a good time. I just bought you the new whip. And now we're on this trip that I'm spending all of my money on. You seem real ungrateful!"

"Well at first I was excited about everything Chauncey."

"So why are you having a change of heart?"

"I don't know if I should say anything, it's really none of my business. And I don't want anyone getting angry, so I'll just leave it alone."

"Yo hold up."

Sheila stopped in her tracks.

"Aye, why don't y'all get some snacks or something?" He pulled out some cash and gave it to Cartier. "Go get something to eat for you and the boys while I talk to Sheila."

"That's what I'm talking about, thanks pops!" Cartier and the other boys ran towards the concession stands.

Chauncey led Sheila over to a park bench and they both sat down. "Yo, tell me what's on your mind Sheila. I don't know what you trying to say, but you really need to just say it so we can talk about it and move on. I know me and Sasha didn't work out, and we weren't there for you, but we're here now! I'm here and your mom is coming back to Cleveland. Damn can we at least get some credit for that?!"

"Chauncey what are you talking about? This has nothing to do with that! Look, I appreciate everything you've done for me. You need to know that first and foremost! And I know it's not my place to speak on this, but I really don't like how you treat Candy!"

Chauncey stared at Sheila with a perplexed face as if she had said something strange to him. "Yo, what are you talking about? What you mean you don't like how I treat her?! How am I treating her?"

"Well last night, Candy was really upset about you not being there and how you just left!"

Chauncey laughed aloud. "So that's what happened, last night y'all were up talking about me? Yo, you can't let people manipulate you Sheila, you only hearing one side of the story. You don't know what goes on with me and Candy. And like you said, it's not your place to speak on anything concerning me and her." Chauncey was becoming irritated and felt like Sheila was out of line for bringing up the conversation.

Sheila stood up from her seat. "Ok, well then what about this seventeen year old that you were supposedly dealing with?"

"Yo, Candy really told you that shit?!"

Sheila became fearful of him at that moment. He was very intimidating and the aggression in his voice showed that she may have opened up a can of worms. "Yeah she did, but she was really hurt last night, and I think that -"

"Yo, where Cartier and the boys at? We're about to leave." He frantically got up and began searching for the boys through the crowd of people near the concession stands.

"Wait, what do you mean we're leaving, we just got here! And aunt Trina isn't even back yet!"

"Nah, this trip is definitely over. Your aunt will be fine. I'll call to let her know we can't stay."

Sheila was nervous, she didn't think that her father would respond this way. "I wish I wouldn't have said anything!"

"Yeah well that makes two of us Sheila."...

20 minutes later Chauncey sped into the parking lot of the hotel. He pulled up to valet and told everyone to stay in the car until he got back. Then he quickly rushed into the hotel. Once he reached his room, he went inside and furiously slammed the door.

"Candy!" He yelled out as he walked through the hotel room in a rage. Candy came running out of the bedroom, in fear that something had happened from the tone of his voice.

"What's wrong, where are the kids, is everything ok?!"

Chauncey quickly grabbed Candy by the arm. "Why the fuck did you tell my daughter about that girl!" He pushed her down on the couch and stood over her.

"Chauncey, what are you doing?!" Candy cried out.

"What am I doing!? Nah, the question is what were you doing?! Why would you tell my daughter about one of the lowest points of my life?! Are you trying to purposely ruin my relationship with her?!"

Candy sobbed miserably, she couldn't control herself. "Chauncey I'm sorry, I was just hurt and got caught up in the moment!"

"Candy, pack all of yo shit, we going back to Philly!"

She stood up and tried to grab his arm, but he yanked away from her.

"Get the fuck off me!" Then he stormed out of the hotel room, slamming the door behind him as hard as he could...

***

Everyone arrived back to Philly the next day. It was a long car ride back home. Sheila felt like she was sitting in solitary confinement. No one talked to each other. Soon as they arrived back to Philly, Chauncey had already booked a flight for Sheila to return to Cleveland. He checked himself into a hotel. It didn't look like he was going home with Candy anytime soon. Sheila stayed at the hotel with him until it was time for her flight to depart...

Later that evening, Chauncey and Sheila arrived at the airport. He put his Suburban into park and turned off the ignition. "Yo, I know everything got cut short, but it's a lot going on that you just don't understand right now. The trip got all fucked up because Candy wanted to be in her feelings over some dumb shit." Chauncey was clearly still upset. He looked down at his watch, realizing Sheila only had fifteen minutes before she had to board her flight. He got out of the truck to open the door for her. "Come on, you can't miss your flight." As soon as she stepped out, she gave him a hug. "Yo, you still my little girl." He kissed her on her forehead. "You got all your bags?"

"Yeah I do." Sheila walked away and went inside the airport to board her flight. Chauncey watched her until she was out of sight...

***

Sheila was talking on her cell phone with Nora while driving to work. Her grandparents weren't happy to hear about how everything ended with her trip. And it put a sour taste in their mouth about Chauncey all over again. Sheila didn't tell them the real reason why they left Florida early. Instead she told them Candy had gotten sick. But Nora kept going on and on about how something just didn't sound right about the whole story. "Ma, I still had a good time, plus I got to meet a lot of family!"

"That's great Sheila, and I understand Candy was sick and all. But why would you have to come home early because of that?"

Sheila knew she needed to end the conversation quickly, because clearly Nora wasn't going to let it go. "Ok Ma, well I just pulled into the parking lot at work, so I'll see you when I get home ok?"

"Ok baby," Nora said as she hung up the phone. Just as Sheila was turning into the parking lot of her job, she was cut off by a guy driving a long four door Lincoln. It looked like a piece of crap and Sheila was furious that he had nearly hit her car. She hurried to pull into a parking space, in an attempt to see who the guy was that almost hit her. But to her surprise, he was already getting out of his car and walking towards her. The guy tapped on her window once he approached her car. Sheila rolled it down slightly. "Yes?"

"Hey Ms. Lady, I'm so sorry! I almost hit you, I didn't even see you coming, are you ok?!"

"I'm fine, let me step out of the car ok?"

"Oh yeah, yeah of course!" The guy stammered over his words as he opened Sheila's car door for her. He was tall, handsome, and brown skinned with a low cut fade. "Aye, you gorgeous!"

She laughed at how serious he looked while complimenting her. "Well thank you."

"Look, I know I just almost wrecked your car and all, but you should let me take you out, so I can make it up to you."

Sheila laughed again, this guy was hilarious and she loved his sense of humor. "Well, I'm seeing someone right now, so I don't know if that would be a good idea."

"Oh I understand that, I'm not trying to step on anybody's toes. But it's the least I could do, especially since I almost killed you!"

Sheila couldn't get enough of his humor. And she found him very intriguing.

"By the way, my name is Antonio, what's yours?"

"My name is Sheila."

"That's a pretty name, it fits you. You should let me get your number though Sheila, so we can just talk sometimes."

"I guess that's ok, just to talk."

He gave her his cell phone and she put her number in it. "Alright Ms. Sheila, I'll be talking to you soon."

"Ok," Sheila crossed the street and went to work. Antonio watched her walk away…

Soon as Sheila got into her job, she was met by her manager who clearly had something he wanted to say to her. "Sheila, can I see you in my office?"

"Sure," She responded, wondering in her mind what her manager could possibly want to speak with her about…

"Sheila, have a seat please … Look, there's no easy way to say this. But we just did our annual report, and unfortunately we're going to have to do some major cutbacks, starting in your department."

"Ok, so what does that mean for me? Are you going to cut back on my hours, I barely get twenty per week now!"

"Sheila I'm sorry, but we're going to have to let you go."

"What, let me go, but why?!"

"Well Sheila, it's all based on seniority. And with you still being a minor and only working here for six months, it just wasn't enough longevity to secure your position."

"This is crazy, I've got prom coming up and I need all the money I can get right now!"

"Again Sheila, I am truly sorry. Maybe you can try to reapply in the summer when business picks up a bit?"…

***

"Your manager is an ass hole!" Sheila went over to Deborah's house after she left work and told her what happened. "Don't worry, you'll find another job soon. I heard that BW3's is hiring, maybe you should try there."

"Really? I'll have to look into that tomorrow. I need money for prom!"

"I know that's right girl!" Deborah walked across the room and retrieved a letter from her China Cabinet. Then she gave it to Sheila, it was a letter from Ryan.

"Wow I haven't gotten a letter from him in months!"

"Well, you might not be too happy to read what you're about to read."

"Oh goodness… but wait, why is it already opened Deborah?" Sheila looked on the front of the letter and noticed that Ryan had addressed the letter to Deborah. "Did he purposely send this to you?"

Deborah shook her head. "Open it up and look at the second paragraph on the second page."

Sheila opened the letter and began to read it…

I saw that picture Sheila sent me with you in it, and damn! You look good as fuck, way better than Sheila! I don't want her, what's up with me and you? I only got three years left. I'm trying to be with you when I get out, so what's up? …

Sheila couldn't believe her eyes and what she was reading. "What in the fuck, is this nigga really trying to get with you from jail?!"

Deborah lowered her head in shame.

"Damn, this is a fucked up day! First I lose my job, and now my man wants to be with my best friend!"

"Girl, you do not have to worry about me, I don't want that boy!"

"That's not the point Deborah! I can't believe this, wait until I show Lashonda this shit!"

Sheila attempted to fold up the letter and put it inside of her purse. But Deborah quickly took it from her hand.

"What are you doing?"

"What were you about to do with the letter Sheila?"

"Um, I'm putting it in my purse so that I can take it with me?!"

"You can't take it with you."

"What do you mean I can't take it with me?"

"Sheila, he wrote the letter to me, it's not for you. I just wanted to show you what he sent me so that you could see what he's up to."

Sheila immediately stood to her feet. "So you're seriously not going to give me the letter? What the fuck, are you interested in Ryan or something?"

Deborah began to laugh, and it infuriated Sheila. "If I wanted him, I could have him Sheila. I just think you're over reacting over a letter."

"Ok Deborah, you keep the letter. But that's really some shady ass shit to do!"...

***

"Let's see here, so you worked at Top's supermarket for six months?"

Sheila went to BW3's to put in an application for employment. She lucked up and got an interview the same day with the manager. "Yeah, they were doing some downsizing in my department, so I was let go."

"Oh I'm sorry to hear that... So if I hire you when can you start?"

Suddenly, another man came into the office. He was a young light skinned guy with a nice muscular body.

"I can start as soon as possible!"

"Well that sounds great. I'd like for you to meet the other manager on duty. Sheila this is Everett, Everett this is Sheila. She's the new cashier and she starts Monday."

"Hey Sheila, it's nice to meet you."

"Thanks, you as well."

"Everett is the night manager, so you'll be working on his shift."

"Oh ok, great!" Sheila couldn't wait to get started. Plus she'd get to work with a cute guy...

Later that day, Sheila was meeting up with Lawrence for their date.

"Hello beautiful, you look gorgeous baby!" Lawrence was admiring Sheila's fitted little red dress. She had her hair pulled up high in a bun, and wore oversized gold hoop earrings to compliment her look. She could definitely pass for a model.

"Thanks Lawrence," She kissed him on the lips. "So where are we going babe?"

Lawrence didn't tell Sheila where their date would be, he just told her to dress up. "It's a surprise. I think you're going to like it a lot." He took her hand and kissed it gently…

Sheila was mesmerized by him more and more as each moment went by. About half an hour later, they arrived at a boat dock downtown. "Wow a boat ride Lawrence?!" Lawrence had rented out an entire boat for them to have dinner on, and it was just the two of them. She couldn't believe it. "Lawrence, no one has ever done anything like this for me before!"

"Well you deserve it." He took her by the hand and led her down the dock and onto the boat. There was a romantic candle lit dinner prepared for them…

After dinner, they went back to Lawrence's place. "You've just got our night all planned out don't you?"

"You could say something like that." Lawrence pulled Sheila by her waist and kissed her passionately. She wrapped her arms around his neck while gazing into his eyes. "Sheila, I just want you to know that I really do love you. I feel like we have a true friendship above anything else, and that means a lot to me."

"So do I Lawrence. I don't want this night to ever end, it's like a dream."

"I know it is beautiful." Lawrence whispered in her ear as he kissed softly on her neck. Then he picked her up and laid her down on the bed. He straddled himself on top of her while continuing to kiss her. All while running his hands up and down her thighs. And cuffing and gripping all of her ass with his hands.

Sheila started grinding her pelvis against him. Then she grabbed his face and looked him in the eyes. "I want you to be the one, I want you to make love to me." Lawrence laid his head down on her chest.

"Are you sure this is what you want? I'm not trying to force you to do anything."

"I know that Lawrence. We've been dating for a while now, and you're very special to me. I wouldn't want to give myself to anyone else, I love you."

Lawrence stared into her eyes and kissed her again. Their tongues devoured the taste of one another's. He stood up, anxiously pulling his shirt over his head. Then he pulled down his pants and underwear. His naked body was standing in front of Sheila, waiting to take and penetrate her. Looking at his dick made her scared. She didn't know if she would be able to take it all in or not. It looked at least ten inches long. It was thick with veins bulging out the sides of it. And the tip looked like the perfect mushroom shape. He lied down on top of her, and slowly pulled her dress off. Lawrence kissed every inch of her naked body. Then he slowly slid her panties down.

"Wait Lawrence, I'm a little scared."

"Sheila, don't you trust me?"

"Of course I do."

He took his finger and stroked her clit, making her vagina drip like a leaking faucet. Then he put his finger inside of her vagina, searching her walls from side to side in a circular motion. Trying to make room for himself to enter, all while sucking her breast and caressing her body. He felt her climax on his hand, so he pulled his finger out and put it inside his mouth, tasting her love. "Damn baby, you taste so good." Sheila moaned intensely. He grabbed his dick and rubbed it against her pussy, making her almost climax again. Sheila was on a sexual high at this point. Then he tried to slide his dick in slowly, working the tip of it in first.

"Ouch, that hurts so bad Lawrence!"

"Relax, I'm going to take it slow." He moved his dick in and out slowly, inch by inch, breaking down the walls of Sheila's virgin pussy. He finally got all the way in, stroking in her slippery wetness. They were making love, and she was becoming a woman…

Lessonz Learned

Lawrence took Sheila back to her house around 5 a.m. Nora and Frank both worked the night shift, so they wouldn't get home until six or later. Sheila was feeling an array of emotions and was silent on the entire car ride home. It was almost like she wasn't the same girl anymore. She felt different and more physically connected to Lawrence...

"This night was so special to me. I feel like my whole life has changed. I just gave you my virginity! So what happens between us now?"

"What do you mean what happens now?"

"Well, we've been dating for six months, and you just took my virginity. Doesn't that mean things between us are more serious?"

"Sheila, you're very special to me, can't you tell? I went out of my way to make this night and your first time special, didn't I?"

"Sure Lawrence, I know that. But we've had some really deep conversations. Remember when you told me that you wanted to be married and have kids? I guess I thought we were on the path to having that one day. Was I wrong?"

"Whoa, slow your brakes now Sheila! Of course I want all of those things. One day when I'm older, not right now! We're both really young and you're not even out of high school yet! You've got a lot of experiences to have and I wouldn't dare try to tie you down and take any of that away from you!"

All this time Sheila thought that Lawrence wanted the same things she did. But maybe she was mistaken. "What was the point of you telling me not to talk to any other guys then? And telling me that we were exclusive?!"

"We are exclusive Sheila. When I'm here in town, I'm here with you only."

"What do you mean when you're in town?! What about when your ass is out of town?! I just gave you something so precious to me! Something I told you I would only give to a man that would be my husband one day!"

"Look Sheila, I'm young right now, and my career is just taking off. I've got one more year of college left! I'm trying to really establish myself and I don't see how I can fit a wife and kid into all of that anytime soon!"

"So I guess you're going to tell me that you're not taking me to prom either right?"

Lawrence looked away and stared out of his driver side window. As if he were suddenly interested in the scenery outside. "Yeah, about that, I checked my calendar and my exams are on the exact same date as your prom! I really had no idea when I agreed to take you. I swear I didn't, honestly I- !"

{Slap} Sheila let her right hand fly right across Lawrence's face. She had enough and felt like he had taken advantage of her vulnerability. She got out of the car and slammed the door.

"Hey, what in the hell is wrong with you?!" Lawrence got out the car next, in an attempt to catch up with her.

"Don't you come anywhere near me! Get away from me Lawrence!"

"Sheila, you're over reacting! Let's just get back inside the car and talk! You've got everything all misunderstood baby!"

"I'll never talk to you ever again in my life you fucking liar!" Sheila hurried inside the house. Lawrence got back into his Buick and angrily sped off...

After a long hot shower, Sheila dried off and put on her favorite fragranced lotion. Then she slipped into some boy shorts and a white tank top. Her heart felt like it was beating a million beats per minute and her mind was racing. Suddenly she heard a knock at the door. It was almost 7a.m. She wondered who could possibly be knocking at the door this time of morning. She looked out her bedroom window, trying to see if there was a car parked in the driveway. Then she heard knocking again at the front door. "Who is it?!" She yelled out from her bedroom window. Then she saw a shadow of what appeared to be a woman. She was tall and thin with long hair and a brimmed hat pulled over her face. Instantly Sheila was frightened as she didn't know who the woman was. Then the woman came into clear sight and made eye contact with Sheila.

"Sheila it's me, Sasha." ...

Sheila ran out of her bedroom and down the stairs to open the door. Surprisingly, she ran to her mother as if she missed her dearly. She squeezed her tightly and Sasha hugged her back just as tight. Mascara ran endlessly from Sasha's crying eyes. "Sheila honey, oh my baby, I've missed you so much!" Sheila immediately burst out into tears. She had so much resentment towards her mother for not being there over the years. But now all she could think about was how happy she was to see her.

"Sasha, I missed you too!" Sheila took a moment to stare at her mother, and she could see that life had really been rough on her. First she looked at Sasha's frail body. Then she noticed that the pigmentation in her lips was severely discolored. And she smelled like alcohol. Sheila's heart hurt badly for her mother. All she wanted to do was nurture her at that moment. "Come on, let's go inside Sasha!" Sheila led her into the house.

"Sasha, I wish we knew you were coming, Mama and Daddy are still at work!"

"Well, I really wasn't planning on coming, but life brought me so here I am." The more Sheila examined her mother she saw that Sasha didn't look well at all. And the cheap blonde wig she wore gave her the appearance of a prostitute. "Sasha, you have to stay here and get yourself together, you have to! Mama worries sick about you all the time!"

"What about daddy, does he worry sick about me too?" Sheila put her head down. She knew of the ill feelings her grandfather still had towards her mother. "I guess some things will never change!" Sasha got up and began to walk around the room. Then she stopped to stare at all the pictures sitting on the fireplace mantle. Suddenly, she recognized a picture of Denise holding a diploma and wearing a cap and gown. "I always knew she was going to be the one to do something with her life."

Sheila got up and stood next to her mother. They both stared at the picture. "Yeah, auntie is doing great!" She has her own medical practice down in Tampa Florida. But we don't get to see her that often. She works crazy hours in that sort of field."

"I'm not surprised. What type of practice does she run?"

"Oh, she runs an OBGYN clinic for pregnant women... So Sasha, what have you been up to? It's been a long time since I last saw you, are you back with Mark?"

"Please, that bastard?! I will never talk to him again! He ruined my life, and he took me away from you! You're the only thing I've ever cared about, and he took that away from me!"

Sheila looked away, almost in disgust at her mother. "A man can't take you away from your daughter Sasha that sounds ridiculous."

Sasha rose from her seat and approached Sheila. "So this is what we're going to do, point the finger and play the blame game?"

"Hey, you brought up the subject! I don't know what the point is of you mentioning anything from the past about you not being there for me!"

"Well Sheila you know what, I'm here now and I want to be in your life! The question is will you allow me to be in it?"

Sheila didn't view Sasha as a mother, but more like a distant relative. She didn't even know Sasha's favorite color, her favorite food, or what she liked to do. Sheila felt like she knew more about a stranger on the streets than her own mother.

"Look Sasha, I don't know what you want from me, or what you're expecting. But I don't have any ill feeling towards you, ok? Seriously I don't!"

"Sheila, let me tell you something. I don't want anything from you! I'm the giver in this situation, I gave you life! And I've given you much grief and distress as well. And for that, baby I'm sorry! I was just in a really messed up place, dealing with all the wrong people and hanging in all the wrong environments! I put my trust in people that didn't care about me! They only wanted to use me for what they could get out of me, especially men!" Tears began to fall from Sasha's eyes. "And Sheila even after all these years, the only thing I could think about was you! Thinking about how I didn't want my daughter to go through any of the bull shit and drama that I did! I've prayed to God and asked him to shield you! Shield you from evil men, drugs, and abuse! You have no idea what horrible things your mother has done! I'm completely polluted from the world! Baby mommy is so tired, do you hear me?! I'm tired! Sheila, if you remember one thing from me, remember to never allow anyone to use you! Baby you are a precious gem, a ruby surrounded by tons of dirt! Honey I've dealt with many men, from rich, to middle class, and even poor men. And in all my years of living, I can honestly say that no matter if they were rich or poor. If their heart isn't right, then that man isn't right!"

"Sasha, I understand you've made some bad choices ok, really I get it. But I'm a strong woman, and not to be disrespectful, but I'm not weak minded like you."

"Weak minded?! Ok, let me ask you this, are you still a virgin?"

Sheila was completely caught off guard by the question. And the fact that she just lost her virginity hours ago wasn't helping the situation. "Well, judging by the look on your face, I'll take that as a no. So tell me, where is this guy that took your virginity?"

"Sasha, you can't just barge into my life demanding to know all of my personal business! You haven't even been here for me over the years. You've never been here, and you never cared about me!"

"My god, please have mercy on my child! For her parents have forsaken her, and now she seeks love in places she can only get from you lord." Sasha was on a rant. As if she was talking to someone who wasn't even in the room.

"Umm hello, what are you talking about?"

Sasha shook her head. "Soon my love, you will come into the truth, all in due time. Sheila my heart hurts for you! The evil deeds that your father and I have done had a serious affect on you! And in my spirit, I sense that you are out here seeking love in all the wrong places! So please listen to your mother, and hopefully this can be a lesson learned to you. Only God can truly fulfill you and satisfy you! You're not going to find happiness or peace in anything else except him. I have done things that I will be ashamed of until I go to my grave and meet my heavenly father. So I need you to learn from me, your mother. You think that it's impossible for you to do the bad things that I've done? Well Sheila it's not! And I don't want the same lust demon to follow you that's been following me for the past twenty years!"

"Alright Sasha," Sheila kissed her mother on the cheek. "I will think about what you're saying."

"Sure you will, just not right away. And I hope it's not too late by the time you do." Sasha headed for the door.

"Wait, where are you going?"

"I have some things to take care of, I can't stay Sheila."

"But you haven't seen Mama and Daddy yet?!"

"Sweetheart, everything will come together in time. And I'm sure you won't forget to inform them of my visit." She hugged her daughter tightly and kissed her on the cheek. "I love you Sheila, I always have and I always will! You are me and I am you, remember that. I'll see you soon ok?"

"So you're just going to leave? But it's still dark outside!"

"Baby, people walk in darkness everyday while they're in the light and don't even know it."

Sheila watched her frail bodied mother walk away from her. It felt like she was being left on top of the kitchen table all over again...

***

It was finally the weekend. Sheila, Lashonda, and Deborah were downtown doing some shopping. Afterwards they ate pizza at the food court inside the mall.

"Girl, all this damn walking got me tired and hungry!"

"Well it isn't like a little walking wouldn't help you Lashonda." Deborah laughed at her own joke.

"Bitch, shut your skinny ass up!"

"Y'all are silly as hell." Sheila chimed in.

"Girl I still can't believe what that nigga Lawrence did to you! That shit wasn't right at all, he just got what he wanted and left!"

"Yeah he really did." Deborah agreed with Lashonda.

"Both of you need to shut up! Lawrence is not a bad guy and he didn't play me! I guess we just want different things out of life."

"Yeah, well he sure didn't want something different when he was in between those thighs, y'all were very likeminded then!"

"Oh whatever Lashonda! You don't even talk to the dude that took your virginity! And Deborah lost her virginity to a gay dude so that shit doesn't even count!" Sheila and Lashonda laughed out loud.

"Bitch Jonathan is not gay, he's just metro sexual!"

"Deborah, did you just say metro sexual, what the fuck is that?!"

"You know what it is Lashonda! When guys like to dress extra nice and shape their eyebrows, get manicures and pedicures. They're just more in tune with their feminine side, that's all."

"Nah, I don't know what that is! Arching your eyebrows isn't being masculine at all!"

Suddenly, a tall brown skinned guy approached their table. He was wearing a Coogi set, Timberland boots, and glasses with gold frames. The girls stopped talking soon as he approached them.

"Hey ladies, how are you?"

"Hello," the girls all replied in unison. The guy chuckled at their response.

"Do we know you?!" Lashonda clearly had an attitude. Instantly taking away any upper hand the guy thought he had.

"I'm sorry sweetheart, you don't know me. But I saw your friend and I just couldn't take my eyes off of her." He was referring to Sheila.

"This bitch always get the cute dudes!"

Sheila nudged Lashonda on the arm. "Girl shut up!"

"Come on Deborah, let's go while he talks to Sheila and get her phone number."

"What?! We're all leaving together, I'm not staying here to talk to anyone."

"Damn it's like that?" The guy asked.

Sheila looked at him. He was really handsome, but she didn't want to get caught up with anybody new because of what happened with Lawrence.

"Look, you seem like a really nice guy and all, but I have a lot going on. And now just isn't a good time for me to meet anyone new."

He extended his hand to Sheila, motioning for her hand in return.

"What are you doing?"

"Give me your hand."

Sheila was hesitant at first.

"Girl just give the man your hand damn!" Lashonda blurted out from across the table.

"Girl shut up, I thought y'all were leaving!"

"Oh so now you want us to leave?! Come on Deborah, let's not disturb the two love birds." The girls joked as they walked off.

"So, can I have your hand please?"

"This is so silly." Sheila gave him her hand.

He took her hand and kissed the back of it. "Hello, my name is Juan, and you are?"

Sheila was flattered but didn't want to show it. "My name is Sheila, it's nice to meet you Juan."

"Like I said Sheila, I couldn't stop staring at you from across the room. So I had to be a gentleman and come over here to properly introduce myself."

"Well I'm flattered but -"

"I do parties, I'm a DJ and I dance."

"Oh you dance, what type of dancing do you do?"

"It's called Breaking."

"Breaking?"

"Yeah breaking, promise me you'll come to my show next week and check me out? I'd love to see you there."

Sheila thought about it for a moment. "I don't see why not. I can bring my friends too right?"

"Yeah, of course you can." The two of them exchanged phone numbers…

***

Sheila and Deborah had plans to go on a double date later that night. It was with the guy Antonio she met in the parking lot of her old job last week, after he had nearly hit her car. She had been talking to him on the phone for the entire week. Surprisingly they had great conversations and spent hours talking. He was a rapper and he was doing a show at one of the local clubs in the city. He had a friend that was performing with him named Raphael. So he asked Sheila to bring one of her friends so they could all hang out after the show. Sheila and Deborah pulled up to the night club in the black Benz that Chauncey bought for her. They were dressed to impress, wearing sexy attire as usual. As they got out of the car to stand in line and get in the club, all the guys were nearly gawking at them.

"Damn!" A random man blurted out as he approached them in the line. "My goodness, now I'll admit, I've seen some fine ass bitches in my days, but you bitches got it going on!"

Sheila and Deborah looked at each other and were completely stunned. They didn't know rather to attack the guy or just ignore him. Clearly he was drunk from the lingering smell of alcohol on his breath. But before they could do anything, Antonio came bombarding through the crowd of people to get to them. Then he approached the man face to face and furiously yanked him up by his shirt collar.

"Bitch ass nigga what the fuck you doing in my club talking shit to my woman!"

The guy looked terrified, as if he were going to shit his pants or something. "Hey man, hey cuz, I ain't mean no harm man! I just been drinking a little, you know how shit go!" The man was so nervous. But before he could get another word out, two huge security guards snatched him away from Antonio and carried him to the back of the club. One held his arms while the other guard held his feet. The man started screaming to the top of his lungs begging and pleading for the guards to put him down. Everyone outside just acted as if nothing was even going on. It was almost as if that type of thing was the social norm around there.

"Sheila, I thought you were going to call me and let me know when you were coming?"

"Yeah I know, but I was just trying to surprise you Antonio."

"This not the type of neighborhood you want to do surprises in baby." He looked over at Deborah. "Is this your friend?"

"Oh yeah, this is Deborah, Deborah this is Antonio."

"Hey it's nice to meet you."

"Likewise, my boy Raphael is going to like you a lot!"

Sheila and Deborah smiled at each other as he led them inside...

The club was located at the end of town, and it wasn't too far from the projects. All the gangsters and drug dealers hung out there. Rastas, bikers, dope boys, and jack boys, they were all under one roof. It felt like you were walking into a wolves den. Sheila and Deborah practically read each other's thoughts as they looked at themselves and then at the attire of the other chicks in the club. They were dressed in timberland boots and white beaters. And they wore pro model baseball caps, looking like they were ready to stump out any bitch that even dared to look at them wrong. But surprisingly, Antonio seemed to be a very popular guy. Everyone spoke to him and dabbed him up as he walked past. They all seemed to respect him and show him love. Finally, they arrived at the back of the club. It had a short stairway that led up to the VIP room. Once you were upstairs, there was a balcony that overlooked the entire dance floor.

"So what y'all drinking?"

"I'll take a Long Island."

"What about you Sheila?"

"I'm ok, someone has to be the responsible one to drive home."

"Oh ok, pretty and responsible, I like that. Well, I need to go back stage Sheila, we'll hang out after the show with my boy Ralph."

"Ok, sounds good."...

"Girl, if his friend is anything like him then he will be my future baby daddy!"

"Deborah shut your ass up!" The girls both laugh as they sat back in VIP waiting for the show to begin...

After the performance, everyone went back to Antonio's house. Raphael and Deborah seemed to hit it off really well and couldn't keep their hands off of each other the entire night. They were all sitting on the couch watching Menace to Society in Antonio's living room.

"I had no idea that y'all were so talented! I mean you two literally had the whole crowd going crazy. And they were rapping all of the lyrics to your songs, that's crazy!"

"Yeah, it really was a good performance!" Deborah agreed with Sheila.

"We appreciate that, me and Antonio been working hard, trying to make this shit happen for a while now."

"Do y'all plan on going to college or are you going to just pursue your rap career?" Deborah asked, but the guys laughed at her question. Sheila and Deborah were confused by the laughter.

"What's so funny?" Sheila asked.

"Aye, I mean I'm a senior, so I'm about to be done with this school shit. I move shit out here in these streets, just weed and pills. But being in the streets is all a nigga really know. So school ain't for me. I'm leaving that shit to my nigga Raphael."

Deborah focused her attention on Raphael. "So are you going to college?"

"I hoop and shit, so I got a lot of offers to play ball at some different colleges. That's really the only reason why I'm going though."

"Look, y'all some smart girls. And y'all have a home with a family that makes you go to school. Man all y'all bills are paid! Sheila, look at yo spoiled ass, driving around in a Benz, you only seventeen! Where we from, niggas don't come from happy homes."

"Hell nah they don't." Raphael added.

"Where we from, my niggas got to deal with their mom being strung out on dope, and living in welfare housing that's infested with roaches! Mothers selling their kid's food stamps just so they can get high. Y'all know anything about that life?"

Sheila didn't respond to Antonio's questions. Of course she knew all too well about her parents being involved with drugs, but she never experienced anything to the extent of what he was talking about.

"Well, since you speechless right now, I'm assuming you don't know anything about it. Look, a nigga struggling to get a meal and just have clean clothes to wear everyday. So going to college is the last thing on his mind!"

"That's some real shit my nigga." Raphael said as he pulled out a cigar from his pocket. Then he lit it.

Sheila instantly noticed the strong smell of it. It didn't smell like any cigar she had ever smelled. "What type of cigar is that?!"

Antonio laughed as he took a hit of the cigar next. "Raphael, tell Sheila what this is."

"That's weed baby."

Sheila then noticed how their eyes were getting lower, and their body language also became extremely relaxed. She always heard about weed, but she had never been around anyone smoking it until then, and it made her curious…

***

It was Monday evening and school was out. Sheila was on her way to work. She had been working at BW3's for about two months now. Prom was only a few months away, and she still didn't have a date. She started dating Antonio, but she really wasn't happy in the relationship. All he did was smoke weed and rap. They didn't really have anything in common. But she liked spending time with him because he was funny and made her laugh a lot...

"Oh, so I see you're starting your shift a little early today huh?"

It was Everett, Sheila's manager. She couldn't help but to have a crush on him. His deep voice made her melt every time she heard it and she would purposely come to work early before everyone's shift began, just so she could be alone with him. "Well, I didn't have anything else to do so."

"So you come to work early?" They both laugh. "That's not a bad thing, I like that in you. Hey, I was wondering, do you think you could close tonight? Sharon called off so we're a little short staffed."

"It's a school night, I really can't work too late."

Everett stared at her as if he was undressing her with his eyes. "Yeah I know, how about just until eleven? I promise I'll even try to get you out of here earlier than that." Sheila really didn't have to give it much thought. They would be the only two there and she frequently imagined what would happen if he ever tried to come on to her.

"Ok I'll stay, just for you Everett."...

It was the end of Sheila's shift and she was exhausted. Two other employees ended up calling off so she had to do way more work than she anticipated. She was just anxious and ready to get off so that she could go home...

"Everett, I've got everything cleaned up in the back, I'm about to take off and head home now."

"Sheila, can you come here for a second before you go?"

Sheila sighed, he hadn't paid her any attention all day. And every time he did call for her, it was to do something like refill napkins, take orders, or prep food. She was just tired and ready to go. She walked into his office where he was sitting at his desk.

"Sheila have a seat please?"

"Everett, it's so late I just need to -"

"Sheila, just let me talk to you, please?"

Sheila slumped down into her seat while Everett continued to finish typing something into his computer. Then he got up, walked over to the door, and closed it. Sheila wondered what he was up to.

"Look Sheila, there's really no easy way for me to say this."

"What?" Sheila responded. Suddenly she realized that she may have read mixed signals from Everett. She hoped she wasn't about to get fired like she did from her last job. "Did I do something wrong?"

"Something wrong, no not at all. You do everything right, and that's the fucking problem."

"Excuse me, what does that mean?!"

Everett came closer to her while grabbing his dick. He started massaging it through his pants and he was clearly aroused. "Every time I see you girl, in them tight ass black pants, with that apple shaped ass. I just can't control myself!" Sheila stood up at this point. She had a crush on Everett but he was coming on so straight forward and aggressive, she didn't know how to handle it.

"Everett, what are you doing?!"

Suddenly he pulled his dick out of his pants. Pre come was dripping from the tip, and it was hard as a rock. "See, you've never had a man just tell you he wants to eat that pussy, have you? I want to lick all of that pussy Sheila, every bit of it. And I want you to sit on my face while I'm doing it."

Sheila's pussy started to throb. She was horny at just the thought of what he was saying. But she was still nervous as hell at the way he was approaching her, so direct and vulgar. It turned her on and made her scared at the same time.

"Who's taking the time to make that pussy feel good? Who's making that little kitty come, huh? I want to make that kitty squirt." Everett stood there saying all this weird freaky shit to her while stroking his dick with his hand, which seemed to be growing with every word he said. Sheila headed for the door, but Everett blocked her. "Wait, you don't want it?" His dick was just hanging out the zipper opening of his pants, long and thick. Everett's dick looked like it was on steroids. He stared at Sheila with the most engaging eyes. As if he was yearning desperately for her.

"Everett I can't, I've only been with one person. And I have a boyfriend! I've never even been with him sexually yet! I like you too, I just think this is too much and way too soon! And you're my boss, how would that look?!" Sheila tried to talk herself out of the desire but she was weak as hell for him. Her eyes and her body language showed it. He then grabbed her by the waist and began kissing her. Their tongues were in and out of each other's mouths, tasting each other's thirst for lust. Then he put his hands down the back of

Sheila's pants, grabbing her bare ass, and moaning as he did it. He quickly pulled her pants down.

"Everett, we can't do this, we can't!" Sheila was trying to collect herself. She was so horny that she thought her pussy was going to explode. He then picked her up and lied her down gently on the top of his desk. "Just let me taste it then, ok?"

"What?" Sheila said in a confused tone. No one had ever given her oral sex before. He started to rub her inner thighs with one hand, and his penis with the other.

He took his finger and licked it. Then he put his wet finger on Sheila's clitoris and began to rub it. He rubbed it softly and gently to a rhythmic motion until Sheila climaxed. Everett put his finger in his mouth again, as if to taste her. "That pussy taste delicious." Then he grabbed one of her legs and began licking her toes.

Sheila didn't know rather to be grossed out or turned on. He was unleashing something in her. She began feeling extremely freaky and erotic while stroking her toes in and out of his mouth, and letting him play with her pussy at the same time. She had multiple orgasms. He made his way from her toes to her ankles, and up her legs. Then he moved towards her inner thigh, very slowly and strategic, as if taking his time. Finally Everett took the tip of his tongue and licked her clitoris, like it was ice cream on a cone.

"Oh, Everett baby!"

He purposely started talking while licking her pussy. His deep voice sent vibrations through her vagina that made her erupt beyond her control, and her legs shook intensely. Then Everett grabbed her ass and began thrusting her up and down, gliding her vagina across his tongue and his face.

"Tell me you like it."

"I like it!" Sheila yelled out in passion.

He thrust her faster across his tongue, creating wetness that flowed out of her and all over his face. "Say it louder, I can't hear you."

"I fucking love it!" Sheila yelled out as loud as she could, while she continued to have orgasms all over his face for the next hour...

***

It was the end of senior year. And it seemed like it went by too fast. Sheila had so many experiences. She felt a new sense of sexy within herself. Things didn't go too well with her and Antonio, so they mutually decided to break up and remain friends. Everett had become just a one time fling, and they barely interacted with one another at work now. Sheila promised herself that she wasn't going to deal with anymore guys anytime soon. She had been talking to the dancer Juan that she met at the mall. But he was so arrogant and was known by everybody in the city for being a womanizer and a male hoe. Sheila went out with him one time. All he wanted to do was show her the many designer outfits and shoes he owned. It was definitely a turn off because he felt girls were obligated to have sex with him just because of his popularity and who he was. Sheila was fed up with men. She remembered what Sasha told her, and it was really starting to weigh heavy on her mind...

***

It was the night of senior prom and Sheila's date was some random guy she met a few years back. He wasn't her type at all. But none the less he was a good friend that Sheila always confided in when she was having men problems. So she figured he'd be the perfect date for prom. It was disappointing to her because she couldn't go with Lawrence, but she was going to make the best of this night. It only came once. Sheila, Lashonda, Deborah, and their dates all rented a stretch Escalade limousine, and they planned to party the night away until dawn...

"You look so beautiful!" It was Nora, watching as Sheila added the final touches to her look for prom.

She wore a beautiful long flowing red Satin gown that had a gorgeous spread at the bottom. And there was a diamond embroidered neck choker made onto it. The front of the dress had straps that crossed over her breast, exposing the sides of her waist. It was stunning and Sheila looked beautiful.

"That dress is really revealing! But you're eighteen now, you're all grown up!"

"Ah Mama, I'll be fine. I had a shawl custom made to wrap around me so I'll cover up with that."

"It seems like yesterday when you were just a little girl. Now you're a beautiful young woman."

"Ma, don't make me cry, I'm going to ruin my makeup!" The two began to laugh.

"Sheila, I just want you to know that you're about to enter an entirely different phase in life. You're turning into a woman, and with that honey, there comes a lot of responsibility."

"Yes, I know Ma."

"Have you thought about what you're going to do about college? Are you staying in state or are you accepting that offer to Michigan State University?" Sheila was very successful in her academics. She had five different schools from all over the country offering her a fully paid tuition. It sounded exciting at first, but Sheila didn't like the idea of living in dorm rooms with other girls, she was a very private person.

"I don't know yet Ma. I was really thinking about maybe staying here and getting an apartment."

"Now why on earth would you want to do that?!"

"Ma, I just don't know what I really want to do right now, I have so many options! Anyway, its prom night, so can we please talk about this some other time?"

"Of course we can Sheila, but time is ticking and you don't have time to waste. You need to make responsible decisions that won't impact your future in a bad way! You do see what happened to your mother don't you?"

"Yes Ma I know!" She didn't tell her grandparents that Sasha came to visit a few months back.

"All I can tell you is this, most men only want one thing. So you can't just give yourself to any and everybody. Do you understand that Sheila?"

"Ma who said I was?!"

"Well I'm just saying, you're a smart girl with a good head on your shoulders. Make sure you stay on the right track! It's so easy to get off track, but it's hard as hell to get back on it!"

The two of them walked downstairs where Sheila appeared to everyone who was waiting outside to see her off for prom...

***

School was out, graduation was over, and everyone had thrown all the wildest farewell graduation parties. You were either getting ready to leave for college in the fall, staying behind to work a job, or just doing nothing with your life. Sheila had decided to accept a full scholarship to an art institute in the city where she would major in graphic design and business. She figured since art was her love since she was a child, she'd design layouts and do graphics for television productions. College didn't start for another two months, so Sheila was working at the local YMCA in her neighborhood. She loved working with children from the inner city. One group of children she had were siblings. There was one boy and two sisters between the ages of eight and eleven. The grandmother had custody of them because their mother was a dope fiend and a prostitute. And she was always in and out of jail. The grandmother was seventy years old, working part time, and trying to support her grandkids. Sheila had deep sympathy for her and offered to bring the children home for her at the end of each day, since she didn't get off work every night until 7 p.m. And she had no vehicle to pick up the kids. These children had a special place in Sheila's heart because one of them was mentally challenged, and had confessed to her that the older brother was molesting her and her younger sister. When Sheila went to confirm the story with the younger sister, she found out it was true. And the younger sister praised the fact that she performed better sexual acts on the brother than her other sister did.

    Sheila knew it was a learned behavior that the kids had probably gotten from their mother, which is why she tried to help the grandmother as much as she could. She spoke to the grandmother about the situation, and told her that she wanted to offer help so that she wouldn't get reported to child and family services and loose custody of the kids. Sheila taught the kids about healthy and non-healthy relationships. She also taught them not to touch people in their private areas. Unfortunately, right before the end of the summer, the grandmother ended up having a heart attack and the kids went into foster care anyway. It weighed heavy on Sheila's heart for a long time. She realized that most children in the ghetto had horrible living situations and conditions at home. She had another group of siblings at the center, there were four of them. They all had the same father except for one of them. And she looked noticeably different than her brother and sisters because of her course kinky hair. Her siblings were of a lighter skin complexion, and they had a Puerto Rican father. The one child with the black father had a darker skin complexion. Her siblings would tease her about looking different. And the mother obviously treated her differently by dressing her in raggedy clothes. But she would dress the other siblings in much nicer clothes. One day, Sheila took it among herself to get them all together and tell them that they should never go against one another. She explained to them that they were all each other had. And she scolded the three siblings for making fun of the one sibling with the different father. They would tease their sister because of the clothes she wore and the type of hair she had. By the end of that meeting, Sheila had all of those children in tears and hugging one another. They vowed to never tease their sister again. Sheila realized that working with children is what truly fulfilled her. By the end of that summer, she knew one day she wanted to have a lot of kids. And she made a promise to God that she would give them a healthy upbringing if he ever blessed her with any...

The Tragedy

"So what are you saying, you didn't have a good time with me?" It was Juan on the other end of Sheila's phone.

She honestly didn't know why she even still talked to him, he seemed so superficial to her. At first his popularity and good looks intrigued her. But once she got to know him, she knew that she could never date a guy that was so shallow.

"Juan yes, I had a good time! And your show was really good, you can dance your ass off, I'll give you that." Sheila went to a few of his shows that he put on in the city for different events. She always had a good time with him, but she couldn't take him serious. And he always bragged about all the women he slept with around the city.

"So when are you coming to see me Sheila?"

"Why, so you can try to get me naked again?" The last time Sheila went to see Juan, he was anxious to keep her home with him instead of going out to party at the Cotton Club with her friends. He was all over her, but Sheila knew she'd never be intimate with him. Suddenly her other line beeped. "Juan hold on, let me answer the other line"…

"Hello?"

"What's up Sheila?"

It was a deep familiar voice on the other line, but Sheila couldn't figure out who it was. "Who is this?"

"Oh, so you don't know my voice no more?" She immediately knew who it was and wondered what he could want.

"Raphael?"

"Yeah, you busy?"

"Umm no, hold on for a minute." She went back to Juan on the other line.

"Juan can I call you right back?"

"Only if you promise to call me right back."

Sheila sighed, "Yes Juan I will, bye." She quickly clicked back over to Raphael.

"Hey Raphael, what's up?"

"Hey Sheila, I know this a little awkward, but I got something I need to talk to you about. And I really need to talk to you about it in person."

Sheila was hesitant. She knew it was probably nothing that he wanted, but it was Deborah's ex-boyfriend. The two of them dated all senior year and decided towards the end of the school year that they were just going to remain friends.

"Ok, that's cool I guess."

Raphael sensed Sheila's hesitation. "Don't worry I don't bite, unless you want me to."...

It was late in the evening when Sheila got to Raphael's house. He was already sitting outside on the porch waiting for her. He walked to her car and opened the passenger door to get in.

"Thanks for coming through Sheila."

"It's no problem, is everything ok?"

Raphael hesitated to answer her..."No, not really."

"What's wrong, what's going on?"

"Antonio is in charge of the stage performances at the club every week. So he decided to give my spot to another nigga for the rap show!"

"Wait why would he do that?"

"Because he's being spiteful that's why! He starting to realize that he don't got shit going for his life. He's not going to college, so the nigga just miserable! And he wants everybody else to be miserable with him!"

"Raphael please calm down, ok? The two of you have been friends for a long time. And I'm sure Antonio wouldn't do anything to intentionally hurt you."

"Yeah, well you don't know that nigga like I do! I mean, even when y'all was together, I use to tell him that he'd better hold onto you. You're a good girl Sheila. This nigga didn't even want to take you to your senior prom, and that was supposed to be your man, right?"

"Well it's his loss. So I'm not going to dwell on that."

"You right about that, it was definitely his loss... So what are you doing for the rest of the night?"

"I didn't have anything planned, why what's up?"

"You wanna go grab a few drinks, and maybe shoot some pool? I think we could both blow off some steam."

"Are you asking me out on a date? Dude I can't date my best friend's ex-boyfriend!"

"It's not a date though, we just hanging out, that's it."...

Sheila and Raphael ended up spending the entire evening together. They even went to the movies after playing pool. Afterwards they went back to his house...

"That was a lot of fun! I really needed to get out."

"Yeah, you definitely have to do that sometimes in order to regroup Sheila."

"You're right, that's so true! ...Well look, thanks for everything Raphael, and I really think you and Antonio should talk and hash things out."

"That's why I like talking to you. You always stay positive in a negative situation." Before Sheila could respond, Raphael leaned over and kissed her.

She quickly pulled away from him. "What are you doing?!"

"I couldn't help myself. Look Sheila, I'm the one you need to be fucking with. And I really care about you. Like I told you before, that nigga Antonio don't care about you, just like Deborah don't care about me!"

"Wow, this just doesn't feel right Raphael, and Deborah is one of my best friends!"

"So what, me and her haven't been together for a while now."

"How do you think her and Antonio would feel about this?"

"Are you serious, have you even talked to Deborah since she went away to college?!"

"Well no but -"

"No buts Sheila, sometimes people just grow apart. We're both grown, and we can do what we want. I really want you to come inside with me for a while, can you do that?"

"Raphael I'm scared, and I feel really bad about this."

Sheila didn't even know she was attracted to him until that moment. He was very attentive to her needs and she felt like a priority to him the entire night. Raphael got out and walked around to Sheila's side of the car to open her door. Then he extended his hand to help her out of the car. Once she got out, he hugged her tightly while wrapping his arms around her small waist...

***

Hello? Janette, girl wake up!"

"Who is this...Sheila? Girl, its one o'clock in the damn morning! Why are you still up?!"

"Girl, I just did something horrible!"

"Oh no, what did you do now?"

"Janette, I had sex with Raphael!"

"What, Raphael that Deborah use to date?!"

"Yea girl, and I feel so bad about it!"

"Bitch I'm wide awoke now! Why would you do that Sheila?! I mean seriously out of all the dudes that's out here, you chose your best friends ex? That's pretty low!"

"Girl I swear to you I know, and really it just sort of happened! He started telling me all this shit that's going on between him and Antonio. Then the next thing I know he practically declared his love for me!"

"Wait, so he has problems with Antonio and now he's pushing up on you?!" Janette laughed, "Sounds like you might be a pawn in somebody's little get back scheme, don't you think?"

Sheila thought about if for a moment, then she brushed off the thought. "No, it wasn't like that at all."

"Well however it was, you have to tell Deborah, like right now!"

"What? What do you mean right now?"

"You can't go to sleep with some shit like this on your mind Sheila! And the longer you wait to tell her the worse it's going to make things look!"

"I guess you're right, so you think I should tell her tonight huh?"

"Yes you should, I'll click over and call her now."…

"Hello, hey Deborah, were you sleeping?"

"I was almost asleep. Who is this?"

"It's me Janette, and Sheila is on the phone too."

"Oh ok, why y'all wait so late to call me though? I have class in the morning."

"Look Deborah, I have something to tell you. I confided in Janette about it first. And she told me I should tell you right away and not to let any time pass."

"Ok I'm confused, what do you have to tell me girl?"

Sheila took a deep breath… "Deborah, I had sex with Raphael."

"Wait, you what?!"

"I had sex with Raphael, Deborah I'm so sorry! I really didn't mean for it to happen! He sort of just threw himself on me and -"

"And what, you just fell on his dick right?"

"Deborah I told her that was some fucked up shit to do!"

"So Sheila, why y'all didn't call me?"

"What?" Sheila was confused by Deborah's question.

"Why didn't you call me so that I could join in?"

"Deborah, girl what the fuck is wrong with you, this isn't a joke!"

"Look, I have class in the morning. Sheila I'm not mad at all. And you tell that nigga Raphael that I said he aint shit!" Deborah hung up the phone...

***

It was the next morning and Sheila had just gotten up. But before she could get out of bed her grandmother came barging into her bedroom in a panic. "Ma, what's wrong?!"

"I just got a phone call from your other grandmother. Baby Chauncey has been shot several times, and he's in intensive care! He might not make it!"

"What! Oh no, I have to go! I have to get to Philly. I need to see him now!"

"Sheila calm down! Look, let's go over to your grandmother's house and talk to her so we can make some sense of what's going on."...

Sheila and Nora arrived to Jill's house moments later. "Ma, are you coming in?"

"No baby I'm not. You can do this by yourself."

Sheila walked up to the doorstep and knocked on the door. Suddenly, she saw her grandmother appear. She had jet black hair and mocha colored skin. She looked like she was Native American.

"Oh Sheila!" Jill said as she met Sheila at the door. She was barely able to speak through her crackling voice. The two of them hugged each other tightly as if they were never going to let go. "Come in sweetheart." Jill led Sheila into the house...

"I don't know what to say right now, what happened?!"

"Sheila I don't know! I got a call from Candy this morning around 5:45 a.m. I could barely make out who she was at first because she was crying so hard. Then she went on to say that Chauncey went to his shop earlier than usual to open up this morning. And apparently, some thugs were hiding outside waiting for him." Jill started to cry, Sheila consoled her with a hug. "I mean those crooks are just cruel! How can you just plot and scheme on someone like that! They tried to take him away from his kids and family!" Jill was sobbing uncontrollably. "I've got to leave now to see my son. I can't stand not being there with him, I need to know what's going on!"

"So when are you planning to leave?"

"I'm leaving today!"

"I really don't think it's a good idea for you to go alone. You are in no condition at all to be traveling that far by yourself. I'll come with you!"

Jill looked up at Sheila with tears falling from her eyes. "You will?"

"Of course I will! I just have to make sure it's ok with my grandparents but I'm sure it won't be a problem! My grandmother is the one that told me I should come over and talk with you."

"I'm not surprised. Nora has always been a very compassionate and understanding woman."...

Nora and Frank agreed that it was ok for Sheila to go with Jill to Philadelphia. While she was at home packing her things, there was a hard knock at the front door. Someone was deliberately banging as hard as they could it seemed like. Sheila looked out her bedroom window and her jaw almost dropped to the ground. It was Deborah standing outside of her house with four other girls. Antonio was there as well. Sheila quickly decided to call Raphael...

"Hello, Raphael?!"

"What's up Sheila, are you ok?"

"No, no I'm not! Look, I didn't tell you, but I told Deborah about what happened between us!"

"You did what?! When did you do that?!"

"I told her when I got home last night."

"What the fuck! Come on now, I thought this was supposed to stay between us Sheila?! And you didn't even tell me that you were going to tell her!"

"Look, I'm sorry ok, but I really can't explain all of that right now! Deborah, Antonio, and four other girls are standing outside of my house banging on my door! I'm here all alone and I'm scared to go to the door! They might try to jump me!"

"What?! Nobody is about to jump you or do anything to you. Don't answer the door, I'm on my way!"...

Fifteen minutes had gone by, and all Sheila could hear was Deborah and her friends taunting her outside from her bedroom window.

"Come outside you scary ass bitch!" One of the girls yelled out. "We know you in there hoe! You think its ok to sleep with your best friend's ex huh Sheila?!"

"You a fucking slut and this whole neighborhood will know about you now! You nasty ass hoe! Antonio yelled out angrily from outside.

Sheila was worried that one of her neighbors would call the police. Then suddenly, a grey Toyota Camry came speeding down the street and turned violently into the driveway, it was Raphael.

"So what's up?!" Raphael got out of the car exposing the gun he had on his waist band.

"Raphael, how could you do this to me though?" Deborah pleaded as she approached him. "Come on, with my best friend at that?! And why do you have that gun?!"

Antonio rushed to the forefront of the crowd of girls. "So that's what you doing bitch ass nigga? You go kill me over a bitch?"

"Aint shit over no bitch nigga! This shit is about respect!"

"Oh ok, now I see what this shit is about! You feeling some type of way about me dropping you from the show?! And now you wanna push up on my girl?!"

Sheila came running outside. "Look, everybody needs to stop! This is really disrespectful to come to my house with this shit!"

"Bitch disrespectful?! So you think that fucking my man wasn't disrespectful?"

"But Deborah, you didn't seem to have a problem with it when I told you over the phone last night!"

"Bitch that's because she was in a state of shock you dumb hoe!" One of the girls from the group blurted out. "She needed her real friends to talk some sense into her, and you need to be confronted!"

Before Sheila could respond, Antonio threw a sucker punch and hit Raphael so hard that he fell to the ground, knocking his gun from his waist band. It landed inches away from Sheila's feet and she rushed to pick it up. She then turned and pointed the gun towards the angry crowd. Everyone instantly backed away from her. Raphael hurriedly stood to his feet and took the gun from Sheila's hand.

"Wow, so it's like that bruh?"

"We aint brothers no more Antonio! Get the fuck out of here before we have some serious problems!"

"You got it bruh, come on let's go!" Antonio motioned for Deborah and the other girls to leave. They all got into the car and drove off...

Once inside, Raphael tried to calm Sheila down. She was frantic after what had just happened. She was also worried that Antonio would try to come back and retaliate because they pulled out a gun on him. But Raphael assured her that everything was going to be ok. And he promised that he would talk things over with Antonio. Sheila agreed to do the same with Deborah once she returned from her trip to Philly...

***

"This is really bad you know? I mean it's our first time actually spending time together. And it's on the way to see my father in the intensive care unit!" Jill and Sheila were on the car ride to Philly to visit Chauncey.

"I know sweetheart, but hopefully something good will come out of this. I've always wanted a relationship with you. And not a day goes by that I don't think about you or pray for you to Jehovah God." Sheila's grandmother was a devote Jehovah's Witness. She always gave Sheila literature to read about Jehovah and always invited her to come to the Kingdom Hall. But Sheila never wanted to learn about it. And it always made her uncomfortable when her grandmother brought up the topic.

"You know I was raised to be Christian, so I don't know if the whole Jehovah thing would work for me."

"I use to be a Baptist you know."

"Were you really?!"

"Oh absolutely, my mother raised us up to be that way. But you know Sheila, once I started seeing that the Christian Church wasn't teaching the truth about the bible, I had an issue with that."

"What do you mean they're not teaching the truth?"

"Well, witnesses believe in the bible too. But nowhere in the bible does it tell us to celebrate holidays or birthdays. So this is why we don't celebrate them."

Sheila began to get weary of the conversation at this point and decided to change the subject. "Yeah, well you know, I'm always open to learning about new things… Have your heard anything else from Candy?"

"Last time I talked to her she said that he was still in critical condition, he's hasn't responded to anyone yet."…

It was after 10 p.m. when Sheila and Jill arrived at the hospital.

"Yes hello nurse, my name is Jill Taylor, and I'm here to see my son Chauncey Taylor?"

"Yes Ma'am, he's in the ICU in room number 32b. Just take this hallway down to the end and make a right. Then take the elevators to the third floor, and that's where he'll be."

"Thank you," Sheila replied as her and Jill quickly walked down the hallway. Sheila went ahead of Jill and arrived to the room first. When she looked in, she saw Candy and Chauncey's two sisters that she met from Florida. And then her attention was focused on her father. It looked as if he had a million tubes running down his throat. There were all sorts of machines hooked up to him. And his right leg was lifted up in a brace hanging from the ceiling. He looked like he was in the worst possible pain and Sheila's heart dropped as she observed him. Then she looked back to check for her grandmother's reaction, as she felt it may have been too much for her to bare. But before she knew it, Jill had taken one look at her son and instantly fainted…

***

"So it looks like she just has a minor head injury from the fall, nothing too serious. But we still want to keep her overnight for observation, and in the morning she should be good to go."

"Thank you doctor, thank you so much! I figured this was going to be too much for her to handle, she shouldn't have even come!" Candy complained to Sheila.

"Yea you're probably right. I had to convince her to wait and let me come with her. At first she was trying to drive up here all by herself!" Sheila and Candy walked back to Chauncey's room. Once they were there, one of his sisters got up to greet Sheila.

"Hey honey!" It was her aunt Trina and her other aunt Linda. Their eyes were red and puffy from crying over Chauncey. "It's always good to see you. I just hate that it's under these circumstances!"

"I know right." Sheila glimpsed over at her father and cried.

Trina reached over and consoled her. "Baby it's going to be ok. Jehovah God has this under control! We're going down to mom's room. We were just waiting for you and Candy to come back so that Chauncey wouldn't be left alone."

"Ok," Said Sheila.

"Candy, honey you should really go home and get some rest. You poor thing, you've been here all day!"

"Oh I know, but I'm not leaving his side Lisa."

Sheila sat down in the chair next to Chauncey's hospital bed, patiently waiting for her father to wake up…

It was around 8 a.m. that following morning. And everyone had fallen asleep at the hospital watching over Chauncey and Jill. Suddenly, Sheila was awakened by what sounded like a woman's heels hitting the floor as she walked. The sound got closer and closer until the woman appeared in Chauncey's room. She was a short brown skinned female with a pixie haircut, like the singer Toni Braxton use to have back in the day. She was wearing a tight Minnie skirt and high heeled shoes.

"Hello everyone, I'm Rachel, and Chauncey is the father of my child! I have the paternity papers right here to prove it!"

Candy quickly got up from her seat. But Sheila approached the woman before Candy could get to her. "Excuse me, what is all of this about?"

"Who in the hell are you?!" Candy blurted out.

"Candy please sit down, don't make a scene, not here! Rachel please come out into the hallway with me." Sheila led the woman out of the room and into the hallway. Once outside of the room, the woman broke out into tears. "Sweetie who are you?" Sheila asked in a confused but concerned tone.

"Chauncey and I have been together for six months! He was with me the night before he got shot! I just found out about the shooting and I got here as soon as I could! No one even called to tell me anything. I had to hear about this shit on the morning news!"

Sheila couldn't believe what the woman was telling her, and on top of that, she couldn't believe the double life that her father was living. "Look, my name is Sheila, and I'm Chauncey's oldest daughter."

The woman stared at Sheila in shock. "What, you're his oldest daughter?! He told me that he didn't have any kids!"

Sheila instantly felt betrayed and hurt. The fact that her father denied her to this woman made her feel like she didn't even matter to him. "Well, he definitely does, and I'm not the only one. Cartier is my brother and he has five other children!"

"Five?!"

"Look, I don't know ok. My father is just now coming back into my life. And I've only met one of my siblings. I've never met the others. I just know of them."

"This man is a fucking liar and a manipulator! He told me that Cartier was his brother!" She began to break down into more tears.

"Rachel I understand how you feel! As a woman, really I do! But this is really not the time or place to discuss this situation right now!"

The woman was silent for a moment as she thought on what Sheila had just said. "You know what, you're right. Obviously he has been brought low so he can think about some things in his life! You can't just go around lying to people and having your way, karma is a bitch!" She abruptly walked away from Sheila, having no regards. With her hips switching from side to side and her heels clicking down the hospital hallway...

"What in the hell was that about?!" Candy asked Sheila as she entered back into the room. "This man is near death and still manages to create drama!"

"Look Candy, we don't have time to think about anything else! None of this other bull shit matters! Right now, the main concern is getting Chauncey and Jill out of this hospital!"

Candy got up from her seat and gathered her things.

"Where are you going?"

"I'm leaving; I can't even process all of this in my head right now! I don't know what to do, I have to get out of here!" Candy stormed out of the room, leaving Sheila alone by her father's side...

***

"Sheila, is that you?"

She had fallen asleep, but was awakened by a faint whisper calling her name, it was her father.

"Chauncey!" Sheila was so excited that she had to remember not to hug him too tight, she didn't want to hurt him. Tears began to fall from her eyes. "I'm so glad you're awake!"

"What happened, where am I?" He was still shaken up, and he couldn't recall what happened. The doctor warned the family that this could occur. Everyone was instructed to let him gradually recollect his memory on his own. So he wouldn't go into shock from trying to over think things too much.

Sheila tried to make up a lie as to why he was in the hospital. "Oh, well Candy just felt like you needed a check up, plus you hurt your leg pretty bad. But don't worry about any of that, you just sit back and relax, ok?"

Chauncey didn't respond, instead he was trying hard to brainstorm and piece everything together. Sheila noticed this and interrupted his train of thought.

"Are you hungry, can I get you anything to eat, maybe something to drink?"

"Wait Sheila, what are you doing here in Philly? Yo, how you get here?!" Chauncey wanted to know what was going on. He wasn't accepting the answers that Sheila was giving him.

"I'm here with your mom, we both drove up here together to visit you."

"Yo, my mom here, where is she?"

Sheila wasn't about to tell Chauncey that his mother fainted. She was discharged that morning, and had already gone back to the hotel with Trina and Linda. "She's at the hotel. She was a little tired from the drive so I told her to go get some rest."

"Oh," Suddenly, Chauncey yanked his head back onto his pillow, and his eyes started rolling in the back of his head. He looked like he was having a seizure, going into an aggressive compulsive behavior as he spoke. *I aint got it yo, I don't keep it on me!* Chauncey was reliving the shooting in his mind.

"Nurse, nurse," Sheila screamed out for help. Nurses and doctors rushed into the room and tried to sedate him. Sheila stood back watching and crying, in fear for her father's life…

***

It was only one week left before the summer would be over. Everyone was either going back to college or already there. Meanwhile, Sheila was working overtime to save up for school supplies. She had found a new job at a local check cashing place. The restaurant she was working at previously had closed down due to lack of business. Her new job was ok, but Sheila didn't really get along with the other girls that worked there. They were the type of chicks that liked to gossip all day about who was fucking who, or who didn't have the newest whatever. Sheila had no interest in discussing those things. Coincidentally, she used to date this guy named Greg, which was her co-worker's baby father. Her name was Missy, and she thought she was the best thing since sliced bread. But when she found out her man was interested in Sheila, it made her second guess herself. Sheila and Missy even got into a few verbal confrontations at work in front of customers over the matter. But Sheila needed the job, especially so she could save money to visit Chauncey once a month in Philly. He had been admitted to a rehabilitation center. The shooting left him not being able to use his right leg temporarily. And his therapy was ridiculously expensive. He had no money coming in from the shop, and when he got shot, the dudes that robbed the place took most of his savings from his safe. Candy had exhausted all of her resources financially to help keep up with bills and his therapy. This by far was one of the most difficult times of everyone's life, the summer of 2003...

***

"Look, when you come in this house, if it's after ten o'clock at night, you can't go back out!"

"What, that's ridiculous, I'm eighteen years old, and I have a job!" Sheila and Frank were going back and forth about how long she was allowed to stay out. She felt like her grandparents treated her like a child and never gave her any real freedom.

"Ten o'clock is a reasonable time for a young girl to come in the house Sheila! Why do you need to stay out any later than that? The only thing opened after those hours are bars and legs!"

"Oh my goodness, Daddy you're over reacting!" Sheila knew that she had to get her own place if she wanted to be able to do the things she wanted to do. Her grandparents had been over protective of her all her life. Not letting her spend the night over friend's houses, or letting them spend the night over hers. She wasn't even able to go downtown with her friends unaccompanied until she was seventeen. Sheila just had enough of it, and she decided it was time to get her own apartment...

Later that night, Sheila got dressed up to go out. She decided to take Juan up on an offer to come over and watch movies. She really didn't know why she was going, but it seemed like everything was just going wrong and she needed to get away for a moment. When she arrived to his house, she pulled into the driveway and beeped the horn. He came out and motioned for her to come inside...

"Nice house you got here."

"Thanks, it's my aunt's house. I stay upstairs in the attic. Let's go up so we can chill and watch a movie."

"Ok," Sheila agreed. Once they got upstairs to his room Sheila looked around to observe everything. His room looked like the typical bachelor pad. Then she came across the collage he put together of all the girls he slept with from the city of Cleveland.

"You must be so proud of these accomplishments!" Sheila shook her head in disgust at the collage of women.

"No, I wouldn't say proud. I just like to give recognition."

Sheila rolled her eyes as she sat down on the edge of his bed. "So where's the movie?"

He went into his dresser drawer and pulled out a DVD. Then he tossed it onto Sheila's lap. "What the fuck is this?!" Juan laughed at her reaction. It was a compilation video of unnatural obscene sex acts. And there were actually pictures on the cover to accompany the profane title. Sheila threw the DVD on the floor. "I'm not watching that shit!"

Juan sat down next to her. Then he leaned over and tried to kiss on her neck. "Um, I thought we were supposed to be watching a movie?" Sheila objected.

"Why watch one when we can make one?"

"Boy, you better go somewhere and leave me alone, you talking crazy!"

"Why you so tense?"

"I'm not tense at all Juan! I'm just not about to watch that fetish porn or whatever the fuck that video is with you!"

Juan laughed at her remark. "Aye, I got that from my bootleg nigga in the hood, everybody watching it! He got that R Kelly video too of him pissing on that girl! That shit crazy man!"

"No, you're crazy Juan!"

"Nah, I'm just crazy about you. Let me give you a massage."

"I don't know about that."

"What you mean, why not?"

"Boy what are you trying to do?"

"I'm not trying to do nothing. Just let me give you a quick massage." He then put his arm around Sheila's shoulders to get her to lie sideways, which she did. "Come on now, I can't give you a massage while you're lying on your side." Sheila sighed as she turned over to lay flat on her stomach. Juan proceeded to straddle himself across her butt and began rubbing her back.

"Hey, I didn't say sit on top of me!" His body weight created a lot of pressure. It didn't hurt her, but she couldn't move.

"Shut up," Juan said aggressively.

"What?" Sheila tried to turn around slightly, but was unable to fully see him. She put her face down into a pillow and tried to relax. But then she felt him moving as if he was trying to loosen his pants. She turned back around, and out the corner of her eye she could see that he had pulled his dick out. "Juan, what are you doing, we are not about to have sex!"

"But why not?" He asked, as if there were actually a conversation to be had about the matter.

"Dude, get off of me!" He took his hands and grabbed the waist part of Sheila's pants, forcefully pulling them down. "Juan stop!" Sheila yelled out while trying to reach behind her back and pull her pants up. But due to the position she was in, she couldn't get much leverage. Juan finally managed to get her pants down to her knees. Sheila's heart dropped as she couldn't believe what was happening and how fast it was happening. She was still trying to pull her pants up on one side of her leg. But Juan controlled her movements and was keeping them down. She didn't know if he didn't believe her, but at this point she broke down. Choking back her tears, she felt like she had lumps in her throat. "Juan stop, please!" But by then, he had already forced himself inside of her. It felt like he had stabbed her in the vagina. She went num as he thrust himself back and forth, and in and out of her. Sheila began to think to herself. *Why is he doing this to me?! What should I do, should I scream?! But he's not a stranger, I know him!* Her train of thought was interrupted when he reached over and pulled something out of his dresser drawer. Suddenly Sheila felt something being poured on her. He was putting KY jelly on her vagina in an attempt to get her wet. Clearly she wasn't aroused because he had forced himself on her. Then he put his dick back in her, but this time more forcibly as if he were in a hurry. He almost seemed angry. Meanwhile Sheila could only lay there, helpless and lifeless. After a few minutes Juan quickly got up off of her.

"Man, this is the worst pussy I ever had in my life! This shit dry as fuck!"

Sheila hurried to get her pants back on and cover herself. She had so many emotions running through her head. It felt like she was about to faint.

"Man, just get out so I can go get in the tub and jack off. I put lube on that pussy and it was still dry!"

Sheila was humiliated. She hurried out of the house, got into her car, and sped off...

***

"Hey Lashonda, are you busy?"

"Girl no, I just finished unpacking some stuff, what's up? And why do you sound like that?"...

"I just had sex with Juan."

"You what?!"

"I had sex with Juan, and -"

"Girl you are such a hoe!" Lashonda interrupted Sheila before she could tell her what happened. "I mean damn you just lost your virginity to Lawrence, your manager ate your pussy, you fucked Raphael, and now Juan?! Damn girl, give your pussy a break!"

Sheila took the phone away from her ear, trying to hold back her tears.

"So when did this happen?

"About an hour ago"

"Damn that's recent?!"

"Hey someone is on my other line, let me call you back." Sheila made up a lie to end the conversation with Lashonda.

"Yeah ok, make sure you do!"

Sheila sat in her room, in the dark. She wished she could have vented to Lashonda about what really happened. Then she started to wonder. *Am I a hoe?* The only thing she knew for sure is that she didn't want to have sex with Juan. She told him no, but he did it anyway. Sheila couldn't figure out what conclusion to draw from the situation or how to feel. A large part of her felt as if he had taken something from her without permission. She felt like a victim, and she felt violated...

THE END OF

LESSONZ LEARNED SERIES PART 1 of 3

Find out what happens next in Part 2 of Lessonz Learned

"Sheila what happened, why y'all -"
Sheila yanked away from Janette. "Bitch I'm trying to get the fuck out of this house now!" But before she could get any further, Milton was coming towards her with a double barrel shotgun, pointed straight at her head.
"OH MY GOD!" Janette screamed out. Sheila ran to find cover behind Tone. Janette ran towards Milton and tried to push the gun towards the ceiling and away from Sheila. "Milton stop!" Janette pleaded desperately with him.
"Come on man chill out, put the gun down." Tone said nonchalantly with Sheila still hiding behind him.
"Nah, this bitch said she was gone have some niggas run up in here. So have them motha fuckas run up in here then!" While Janette was still pushing the gun towards the ceiling, Sheila managed to run around Tone and darted out of the kitchen door. Milton pushed Janette to the side and went after her. Then Tone ran across the room and tried to block Milton from reaching Sheila. She was frantically trying to unlock the door.
"Milton stop it please!" Janette continued to plead with him. Finally Sheila unlocked the door. All while Janette was right behind her, with Tone behind Janette, whom was still blocking Milton. The entire scene looked chaotic as hell. As Sheila pushed the door opened, she quickly looked back

at Milton to make sure she was out of his reach. But he managed to lean his long body over Tone and Janette. Then he licked Sheila on her for head. It was as if he had gone mad or something. Sheila ran out of the house scared for her life. Janette followed right behind her. Tone came out next, still trying to take the gun from Milton. Suddenly, Sheila stopped running for some reason. She turned around and looked Milton directly in the eyes. He was still pointing the gun at her. She realized that he could kill her at any moment, and it was out of her control...

www.ingramcontent.com/pod-product-compliance
Lightning Source LLC
Chambersburg PA
CBHW052146070526
44585CB00017B/1999